THREE WOMEN AND THE LORD

ADRIENNE VON SPEYR

THREE WOMEN
AND
THE LORD

Translated by Graham Harrison

With a Foreword by
Kris McGregor

and

With illustrations by
Gregory P. Hartnell

IGNATIUS PRESS   SAN FRANCISCO

Title of the German original:
Drei Frauen und der Herr
© 1978 Johannes Verlag
Einsiedeln, Switzerland

Cover calligraphy by Victoria Hoke Lane

ISBN 978-1-62164-359-3 (PB)
ISBN 978-1-64229-106-3 (eBook)
Library of Congress catalogue number 2019949913
Printed in the United States of America ∞

CONTENTS

Foreword by Kris McGregor   7

MAGDALEN
Faith

Unveiled and Yet Veiled   15
Conversion and Discipleship   21
Beneath the Cross   31
To the Tomb   39
The Risen Lord   47

THE WOMAN WHO WAS A SINNER
Hope

Prelude   59
The Pharisee and the Sinner   63
The Parable   72
Forgiveness   85

MARY OF BETHANY

Love

The One Thing Necessary   91

The Meal in Bethany   109

FOREWORD

Maximus the Confessor wrote that "just as soul and body combine to produce a human being, so practice of the virtues and contemplation together constitute a unique spiritual wisdom." Adrienne von Speyr offers this spiritual wisdom in her reflection on the lives of three remarkable female figures from the Gospels—Mary Magdalen, the unnamed sinful woman who washes the feet of Jesus with her tears and Mary of Bethany. Adrienne's contemplation of their encounters with the Lord deepens our understanding of the way God calls us and transforms our lives with the three theological virtues of faith, hope and love.

These pages present more than a "study" of Scripture verses. They bring the reader face-to-face with the living Word of God. Such is the gift of Adrienne's biblical commentaries, which move beyond predictable exegesis. To be sure, certain biblical methodologies are important for the study of sacred texts. Understanding the time, the place and the context of events and characters found in the holy writings is of vital importance. But these

are only preludes to the mysterious encounter waiting for the believer who is drawn into the taber-
nacle of Divine Revelation to meet the Word. It
is Christ who meets the reader, just as he met the
three women brought forward in this book.

Meeting Christ comes about through prayer.
For Adrienne, prayer is a continual disposition of
the head and the heart to do the Father's will and
to receive the Father's self-revelation in his Word.
It is an attitude of availability, which is ever alert
to whatever comes one's way. Adrienne trains the
reader, by her example, to stop seeing things from his
perspective and to gaze upon all things from God's.
With such a paradigm shift, reading a passage of the
Gospel becomes a moment of profound grace. Every
word is important; every action has meaning; every
crumb has enormous sustenance and is precious to
the one who receives it because it is a gift from God.
We are present to the Word, and he is present to us.
This is the Marian attitude of receptivity. The Virgin
Mary, with this awareness, was the first to say yes to
the Word so completely that he entered the world
through her. Adrienne strove to emulate Mary's
receptivity in every area of her life.

One of the hallmarks of Adrienne's commentaries
is that she receives the Word as it is given. During
the Middle Ages, some began to conflate Mary
Magdalen, who was exorcized of seven demons,
with the nameless sinful woman in Luke 7:36–50

and Mary of Bethany, the sister of Lazarus, referring to them as the same person. Some mystical writers, fueled by a pious intention and a holy imagination, put forward writings, viewed as private revelation by the Church, which describe the life and character of this figure. In this book, however, Adrienne receives each woman as given, separately, so that the unique and transformative encounter each one has with the Lord can be given its proper due.

One of the most influential Desert Fathers of the late fourth-century Church, Evagrius Ponticus, said, "If you are a theologian, you will pray truly; and if you pray truly, you are a theologian." With this definition in mind, Adrienne is rightly understood as a theologian. Her prayerful contemplation of the three women leads to a keen understanding of the theological virtues of faith, hope and love. The *Catechism of the Catholic Church* tells us that these virtues are infused into our souls by God and serve as the bedrock of Christian morality. Our ability to live a Christlike life flows from faith, hope and love and gives fuel to our expression of the moral virtues. The relationships of the three women with the Lord give compelling witness to the power of these permeating graces to transform not only individual lives but the entire Church as well.

With Mary Magdalen, Adrienne shows us her lived experience of faith through conversion and discipleship. She grows ever more aware of the reality of the Son's mission, and she, like us, is drawn into it. It is a breathtaking journey the Magdalen undertakes: the captive is set free from the demons that assail her, and she is drawn into the mystery of the Cross, the Resurrection and Eternal Life.

With the sinful woman, we travel the poignant road of hope, which is drawn from penance, mercy and forgiveness. It is important to note that she is unnamed and that we do not necessarily know her particular sins. We are all somewhat anonymous sinners in this world, and Adrienne challenges the reader to see this woman as himself. The woman is redeemed because of her humility, her faith and her hope in Jesus Christ, the giver of new and eternal life. As Josef Pieper wrote, "The Christian strives, in hope, for the total fulfillment of his being in eternal life." Should not we all dare to hope for such fulfillment?

With Mary of Bethany, the greatest of the virtues, love, is exemplified. Her love is generous and strong even in the face of scorn and ridicule. Her love is obedient to the will of the Father, which she has learned from her prayer. And her love is pure, because she loves the Lord alone and with all her heart, with all her soul, with all her strength. Mary of Bethany's response is the Christian call to action, for love shares in the mission of the Son, a mission passed on to the entire Church, the Bride of Christ on earth.

This and so much more are found within the pages of this book, which I highly recommend as a starting place for reading the works of Adrienne von Speyr. And I recommend reading it as she intended: slowly, carefully, prayerfully. That way, the light of Christ will illuminate the verses in such a way that these women will be viewed no longer as figures of stained glass but as vivid personalities whose lives were transformed after their encounter with the Lord.

Kris McGregor
August 15, 2019
Solemnity of the Assumption
of the Blessed Virgin Mary

MAGDALEN

Faith

UNVEILED AND YET VEILED

(Luke 8:2–3)

The Son of God became man in order to be one of us. He is a human being like every other human being, encountering ordinary people and entering into a relationship with them. But at the same time he is the Son of God, one of the eternal Three Persons in God; he is sent by the Father, bearing the Spirit, commissioned with the task of redemption. As such, then, he meets his fellow men in a very special way. Encountering them, he bears and supports them, he takes on what is specific to them and sets them in the context of God. He brings the kingdom of God close to them; he himself is this kingdom. Every person who meets him has been chosen to enter into this kingdom and receive a particular, personal mission. The mission given to him, which he is to fulfil in his existence as a Christian, is already alive in the Son before the person meeting the Son becomes aware of it. The Son is in charge of the whole plan; he knows what is required of each one that the Father may be glorified, that each may have a share in the whole work of redemption.

Jesus' encounters with people in the Gospel seem to be chance occurrences. Individuals appear and disappear; whole crowds of people follow him, witness his miracles and listen to his teaching. Most of them remain anonymous; many come forward only to bring the situation into sharp relief; they could almost be replaced by others. But there are also those who gradually or suddenly come forth out of obscurity and become thenceforward, to the Church's contemplative gaze, the embodiment of some particular form of service to the Lord.

As soon as they come into view we are aware that they have long been the object of the Lord's contemplation and affirmation. He has selected them, adopted them, long before they knew it; and in the meantime, until they emerge from their concealment in him, he carries them. A few of them already sense that one day, perhaps even today, he will call upon them—or even that he has used them already; the relationship between him and them, created by him alone, is not totally unknown to them. But there are, too, those unknowing souls who have encountered him in total concealment, receiving no light; all the same he is carrying them—he carries them for years, shaping their path, guiding them, helping them to become people he will be able to use. From these, who long remain incognito and who also represent the countless number of those whose relationship to the Lord we will never know, we can see with particular clarity the Lord's power by which he can bear every human being within him. He can initiate a relationship with each and every one, a relationship resting, in the first place, on his consent alone. This consent is his creation; this is the way grace operates, preceding every movement and response on man's part. But this consent of his, this Yes to man, already has man's answering Yes within it like a living yet dormant germ; the Lord's unilateral address already bears the bilateral dialogue within it.

Faith tells us that the Mary who said her Yes to the angel had long since been carried in the Son's Yes, even from all eternity. He chose her to be his Mother, he predestined her and, moreover, redeemed her in anticipation. It is as if she is carried by the Son's consent for as long as possible, until the moment of her decision. It is like a person going to confession: he is carried by the Lord's will that he should make his confession until the moment when he actually makes it.

The fact that we are borne up by the Lord does not mean that he simply relieves us of responsibility. Rather, he strengthens us to make the right decision, so that we can come to meet him in the fulness of our free will; we receive the power, from him, to choose what, in him, is the will of the Father.

Mary's whole past is completely contained within her Yes. From it we can see how she has spent her life so far and all the factors that have contributed to shape her consent; we can see how she has shown herself to be capable of being the person the Son desires her to be. And the moment she says Yes, she accepts a responsibility toward him that takes the widest possible account of her own autonomy.

Something similar happens to all who are carried by the Lord, whom he fashions within him, and with whom, sooner or later, he will come face to face. There are two aspects to this carrying, this gestation. One is the eternal aspect, namely, the divine Son's decision, out of love for the Father, to redeem the world. This includes the involvement of the individuals whose mission he has foreseen. The other aspect is that of the earthly life of Jesus, with all its genuinely human encounters: direct encounters, such as when Peter is first introduced to the Lord, and more hidden and mysterious meetings, such as when Jesus sees Nathanael under the fig tree and adopts him, without the latter knowing anything about it.

We do not know when Mary Magdalen was taken over by the Lord in this way. Her earlier history lies in obscurity, but for the Lord this obscurity is full of light; he is acquainted with it, indeed, he fashioned it for his purposes. He knows with certainty all that he needs to know of her. If it remains hidden from us, that is because the Lord wishes it so; it is also to teach us that, in the Lord, all hidden and unknown paths lead to faith. Being carried by the Lord means being drawn to faith. At this particular point in time it is as if there is both all and nothing: in the awareness of the one being carried there is nothing in terms of faith; everything is in the Lord who is the carrier—he nourishes the one in his care out of his own fulness. But as a result of the Lord's action something has happened to this "nothing"; it has been set upon a path, it has already been taken into service.

At some point in the Gospel we come across the name of Mary Magdalen for the first time. She is one of the women who accompany the Lord. She has stepped out of her concealment in the Lord into the visibility of Christian history. It is enough for us to know that, at this moment, carried and sustained by the Lord as she is, her condition is exactly what he needs. A whole history lies behind her as she steps forward. The Lord's carrying of her is his doing; we are not told to what extent Magdalen may have begun to cooperate in this. She appears as one of the women who were the Lord's helpers, and that in itself shows us that, in the Lord, she was already full of light. From now on she will be one of those who are of use to him in his work. But that does not mean that everyone who belongs to the Lord in this way is revealed to us in the same visible manner. That is a matter for the Lord's good pleasure.

Nothing in holy Scripture is unconnected with the Lord. Wherever we come across someone's name in proximity to him, it tells us that yet another person has entered into a common destiny with him. Occasionally the course of events is plain: first comes the challenge to follow him, and thereafter we continue to meet this same name among the Lord's companions. Perhaps we learn some detail of the person's earlier life: that Matthew had been a tax collector, that the others were fishermen. What is mentioned is exactly as much and as little as is necessary to adumbrate the particular manner of the person's election. In other cases nothing is told us of the person's earlier life, but whatever little we are told is sufficient to nourish our faith; by the Lord's power it attains meaning for us here and now, it is charged with eucharistic effect: whatever comes in contact with him is empowered to bring us, too, nearer to him, for it is borne up and energized by him.

CONVERSION AND DISCIPLESHIP

And the twelve were with him, and also some women who had been healed of evil spirits and infirmities: Mary, called Magdalen, from whom seven demons had gone out.... The very occurrence of a name in the Gospel indicates a connection with the Lord, whether the person referred to has come to believe in the Lord or was simply the occasion for some action on Jesus' part; even in opposing the Lord or falling away, the person concerned points to him. There is a kind of ruthlessness in the way Scripture portrays even the most intimate disciples of the Lord, indicating the Lord's divinity more directly, perhaps, than anything else. God alone can appropriate men in such a way, can deal thus with their destiny, their reputation, their dignity, revealing them like exhibits to the Church and the world. The Lord balances this ruthlessness with his redeeming love. Here it is Magdalen who is exposed to public gaze in this way. She is described once and for all as the disciple out of whom the Lord drove seven demons.

Scripture lays no stress on her privilege in being of the Lord's company. It only refers to her deliverance from the demons. Thus she is deeply in debt to the Lord who healed her from her possession. If now he makes use of her in whatever way he will, using her or her money or her time, he has an absolute right to do so. He has delivered her from as many impure spirits as the Holy Spirit has gifts to give. Now, all that she is and has, as a result of being set free by him, is his property. Scripture expressly refers to Magdalen as belonging to the Lord's company. She belongs because she is a possession of his. As a result of the grace of being liberated from the demons, anything in her following of the Lord which might seem meritorious is rendered totally insignificant. To this extent she is like the woman with the hemorrhage who was healed through touching the Lord and now has to come forward and confess it. This confession is not her own merit—but the Lord requires it of her like a confession of sins. It is simply a case of making public what he has done. Both women have come up against a power inherent in the Lord and proceeding from him; they have had the experience of being carried by the Lord and can see its effects on them. All those who encounter the Lord in the way Magdalen did stand in the light of this confession. It is as if their path to discipleship is announced publicly, by way of explanation. We cannot even say that the primary motive in their discipleship is gratitude; there is an incontestable necessity there, springing from the Lord himself, closely related, in this case, to his driving out of the seven demons.

No account is given of how Magdalen was tormented by the demons nor of how she found her way to the Lord. No mention is made of whether she came to the Lord through the mediation of others or whether he simply addressed her directly because from all eternity he had determined to do so. Nor are we told how grateful she was as a result and how liberated she felt; there is no account of how the miracle happened nor whether the demons concerned were those that, according to the Lord's word, can only be driven out by prayer and fasting. There is nothing about all this. Scripture only speaks of service as a result of liberation. And Magdalen remains in this service, although her being with the Lord was bound to mean that she was never to forget the past: she was and is marked by her erstwhile demonic possession. But that is of no concern to her. For her there is only one constant factor: she follows the Lord because he has set her free. Her life is so perfectly instrumental that we are simply presented with her current existence, not with its background nor its development.

... and Joanna, the wife of Chuza, Herod's steward, and Susanna and many others, who provided for them out of their means.... The others who are referred to together with Mary have an easier time, in a way.

Although two of them are named, their past is not exposed. All we know of the rest is that they were among those who served the Lord out of their means; their names are not revealed. Magdalen is the only one to be exposed. It was not her wish; she was singled out by grace. The stain of her past and the grace of her liberation are ineradicably associated with her name. The distance between them gives us a standard, a hallmark—for in Scripture nothing is mentioned in vain. She was possessed by devils, and now she is one of the Lord's most intimate associates. Her past history must be of service in reaching her destination: her demonic possession provides the point of departure for the subsequent manifestation of grace. The distance between these poles is a precise one: the intention here is that grace shall be manifested in such a way that its point of departure is not lost sight of. But the characteristics of this distance can be different: for one person the eternally significant factor is that he was baptized; for another, like Saul, for instance, what is fundamental is that the Lord converted him. What is decisive in the case of Magdalen is that she, formerly the victim of possession, is now privileged to be close to the pure God-man and to minister to him whose Holy Spirit has shown his sovereign power over her impure spirits.

In Saul's conversion we can trace all the various stages: his being blinded by the vision of the Lord, his prayer by night, the sending of Ananias and so forth. We see none of this in the case of Magdalen. Much remains inscrutable, hidden in the Lord by whom she is being carried. No doubt faith grows within her; she is baptized and then takes up her exhausting itinerant life with the Lord. But all this is hidden from our gaze because the Lord has taken over the entire responsibility for it. It is enough for us to know that she has been set free; the rest remains an unspoken mystery between her and the Lord. No doubt her contemporaries knew a little more about her, but what they knew died with them, and it is the Lord who determines what shall be known about her in the Church. This example shows us that even in cases where more is known, where we think we have a certain insight into the soul of a saint and can enter into his conversion process—perhaps through reading his own account of it—there is always much more that is unsaid, known only to the Lord. Between every person and the Lord there is a mystery, and everyone is entitled to privacy and silence. On the other hand it is always up to the Lord to determine and alter the boundaries. According to our way of seeing things the Lord often seems all too discreet in certain cases and almost indiscreet in others. But whether or not we are permitted a glimpse of the former grievous sinfulness of a converted person, the decision rests with the Lord. In the case of Magdalen the Lord has

not thought it important for us to know the details
of her demonic possession; we only need to know
in general that she has emerged from the darkness
into the brightness of faith.

Nor is her faith itself described in more detail.
It is enough that she is with the Lord, in close discipleship. Later, beneath the Cross, her abiding in
the Lord's presence will reveal its effects. For the
moment the spotlight rests briefly on her, as on
some figure in a story—and only the author knows
how the story is going to proceed. The listeners'
excitement is aroused, but it is immediately subdued
by the lack of further information. We do not know
how she feels, how she sees her own past, how she
prays or how she lives her faith. The curtain is raised
on a stage that promises some great forthcoming
action: the tension between the seven demons on
the one hand and her intimacy with the Lord on the
other is so unusual that something highly dramatic
seems imminent. But the scene lacks any definition.
It remains open in all directions, and in the end we
shall see that this openness is the openness of Magdalen's faith, which is stronger than anything. She
will be portrayed as the first person to live her faith
beyond the hiatus of death.

For the present, however, she is close to the
Lord. She is so exposed to his nearness that he can
bring about whatever he wishes within her. She is
presented to our contemplative gaze as a saint, but

in such a way that, while some features are clearly discernible, God veils others, making them totally inaccessible to us. In Magdalen God teaches us not to ask more, not to wish to know more than he shows us. It is part of her effect on us, in God's deliberate plan, that she is described thus and not otherwise. It is extraordinarily important for God that he not simply show us everything, but that he open and close, reveal things and veil them again according to his good pleasure. Magdalen has been handed over to the entire Church and to each one of us; we are free to imagine her life with the Lord in whatever way we wish, provided that it fits with what is subsequently reported. It is not a case of making good or bad "guesses" as to how things may have been; it is not a case of guessing at all, but of a kind of shared experience within a given perspective and direction. We can follow the tracks for a short space, and we know the destination; the path in between is up to us.

Part of the life of the saints is turned toward us; the other and larger part is open only to God in solitude and mystery. This area is closed to psychological analysis. Psychology always acts as if the soul can be exhaustively understood, as if there is no hiding place from the objectivity of its laws. But the nearer a soul is to God and the more it shares a common life with God, the more God covers it with his veil, letting us see only what he wishes us to see.

However, God can also use some jejune text of holy Scripture to lead us further in our contemplation. If a person simply reads Scripture in order to get to know the text as such, the meaning of the words and the sequence and context of events, he will be content with the written word. But if a person meditates on the same passages in a spirit of adoration, laying hold of them not only with his reason but with a concretely lived faith, in thorough determination to seek God and find him, God will often initiate him more deeply into the reality behind the words. Contemplation is not merely a psychological process, it is not the soul's monologue with itself; it is prayer, dialogue with God, in the course of which God's word acts in sovereign freedom. In contemplation God is always unveiling and veiling himself: there is both day and night. Some of the things he gives are brightly illuminated; others are in darkness because God wishes them to remain wrapped in his mystery. But at this stage it is no longer merely a question of human knowledge and ignorance; it is a question of sharing in a specific manner in the way God sees things, as far as he enables us as meditating believers to do so.

God sees everything. If he were to read Scripture, he would not find the least obscurity in any of its words. He would know precisely the way Mary Magdalen believed, prayed and was converted and the shape of her love. God does not just *happen* to be all-knowing; he actively uses his omniscience. It is a part of his love, a form of its expression. For the one who worships and contemplates, love is the way to God's omniscience—in which, as he wills, he allows us to share—but God's omniscience is also a path to his love. The fact that God knows everything must cause the praying soul to love him even more unreservedly.

There is one person who has a special position between the soul and God, namely, the spiritual director officially appointed by the Church. He is commissioned to bring the soul nearer to God; but it is also his task, to a large extent, to represent God to the soul. He stands in a special relationship to God's omniscience. As far as the soul in his care is concerned, he does not possess this omniscience as a gift; yet he is given antennae, as it were, that enable him to see and understand, in faith, as much as he needs in order to undertake the soul's guidance. He has the right to ask questions. He will often need to make up what he lacks in terms of omniscience by asking questions. He can and must make inquiries both of God and of the soul he is directing. He is the only one who can enter into the dark mystery that lies between God and the soul. "What is your faith, your love like? What was your attitude to God at the time? What did God show you?" And since the ecclesial sphere in which this dialogue takes place is essentially the sphere of prayer, of conversation between bridegroom and bride, the soul can safely entrust itself (indeed it must) to the mystery of spiritual direction in the Church, confident of having further light shed upon its life of faith as a result.

BENEATH THE CROSS

(Mark 15:40–41; John 19:25)

There were also women looking on from afar, among whom were Mary Magdalen, and Mary the mother of James the younger and of Joses, and Salome, who, when he was in Galilee, followed him and ministered to him. . . . Standing by the Cross of Jesus were his mother and his mother's sister, Mary the wife of Clopas, and Mary Magdalen. In taking up her discipleship of the Lord, Magdalen had entered into an openness that had no fixed term. Her discipleship was an initiation into faith in which new doors were continually opening. Since God's mysteries are unfathomable and past counting, the initiation itself never comes to an end. Precisely because Magdalen is now so close to the Lord, no end whatsoever can be envisaged. Since he drove the demons out of her and won her for himself, she is now his, and she follows him freely and unquestioningly. But in doing so she is led to the Cross.

There she stands now, together with the other women, including the Mother of the Lord. Through

her own vocation and as a result of carrying her
Child, his Mother knows that she must never stop
accompanying her Son. She will always be the
Son's Mother. When he develops into manhood
and grows away from her, her mode of fellowship
with him changes; perhaps it becomes harder and
more obscure as time goes on, but it is never in
doubt. For her, to be his Mother and to be his com-
panion are one and the same thing. It follows from
the ruthless, inescapable logic of her Yes—a logic
that is self-evident to her. Her consent embraced
it all from the very beginning, and whether or not
she was aware of all the details is immaterial. Her
Yes was unconditional. How could it have been
otherwise, since God himself required it of her?

Magdalen's case is quite different. What she
experiences is not the unfolding of something that
she has willed and affirmed from the very outset.
By driving out her demons the Lord has, as it were,
tripped her up; he has banished evil from her in
order to replace it with his goodness, and he has
done this without asking her leave, simply taking
possession of her in what seems almost like an act of
violence. There was no consultation and no step-
by-step negotiation. The demons had to give way,
immediately, to the Lord's omnipotence. And Magdalen was set free, but her freedom was straightway
requisitioned by the Lord. Perhaps she tried to find
herself again, perhaps she would have liked to know

where she was going now; but instead she found herself so involved in being of service that the very question seemed obsolete. Only one thing was necessary, namely, to follow, to keep going, to accompany him, simply because he had set her free. She is presented with a fait accompli, far more than in the case of the Lord's Mother, and just has to accept it.

But the paths of both women meet at the Cross. And what is humanly opaque in Magdalen's destiny—things spread by way of rumor, things that many people can neither believe nor understand—is deeply known by the Mother of the Lord as she stands here. She suffers, she suffers the most searing pain, but her suffering is secure within her consent, her surrender, her will to go with him. If Magdalen alone had been placed in front of the Cross, she might not have been able to find in it the answer to her life's question: "Why and for what purpose has the Lord rescued me and called me to follow him?" The Cross might have been so terrible, so meaningless to her, as to awaken in her a raging madness. But now she is not alone as she looks up to the Lord who hangs before her; she can also look at his Mother, suffering beside her and, in her suffering, still uttering her Yes of affirmation. She is still alive, despite everything. And the Mother's "despite everything" enfolds all that is unintelligible to Magdalen and wraps it in calm. In the Mother's protective gesture, which,

to Magdalen, immediately becomes the Lord's gesture, she experiences very deeply the meaning of
mediation. We must not miss the Marian aspect
of everything that takes place on Golgotha: it is
all accepted and affirmed, unquestioningly, unpro-
testingly, by the Mother. The unknowing of the
one, the former sinner, is taken up into the perfect surrender of the other, beyond knowing and
unknowing, into the surrender acted out by the
sinless Immaculate Conception.

Magdalen sees the Mother's suffering; she sees
that this suffering is her very own, although it does
not have its center in her. The Mother suffers in
herself because she is Mother, and her maternal suffering comprises both her own suffering and the
suffering of her Child. Such suffering with her child
is part of the mystery of all motherhood; it is not the
child's suffering directly, but it arises in the mother
as a result of the incomparable and unique way in
which her being participates in the being of the child.
In Mary this motherhood mystery acquires a totally
new form because she is a virgin and has conceived
by the Holy Spirit, and because the son born by her
as man is also God. Her suffering resides in the Son,
and his in her, in a way unequalled in any natural
mother-son relationship; this is the archetype—the
unattainable archetype—of all natural relationships. The Son needs the Mother's suffering: not to
lessen his own, but so that his suffering can begin

to be affirmed and taken up by the other believers, so that it can be completed and spread abroad in the Church, according to his predetermined plan. The Mother's Yes, her consent, uttered and lived out, was essential: it was to be an archetype, an example making discipleship possible for the whole Church. The Son needs this suffering in order to show the Father that he is not suffering alone. From the very outset the work of redemption has an open door toward mankind; the Son can go through this door to those who are his and can invite them to come in. He not only redeems believers, he incorporates them into his work as collaborators. Through the door that is represented by the Mother, the grace of the Cross gives to men a new form of merit. To those who are gathered around the Cross the Son gives the perfect grace of redemption which he won in his dereliction there; this work of redemption comes to them, as to everyone, without the slightest merit on their part, yet he allows them a unique participation in it in which merit does actually accrue to them.

So Magdalen recognizes that she too is involved in this new mystery, with its densely veiled uniqueness, that unites Mother and Son. At the moment all that is required of her is simply to be there with the other women who, like her, have shared the Lord's itinerant life; all she has to do is join with them in contemplating the dying Son; somehow, she does not know how, he is involving her in a new mystery of participation. She yields—it is hard to say how far she does so freely and how far she is drawn against her will—sensing nothing and yet sensing something through the Mother. She does not understand, but something of her unknowing is held within the Mother's comprehension; she suffers as well as she can, as far as it is given to her, but the suffering that penetrates the center of her soul draws her out of herself and into another center, into the mystery of the Son and his Mother. She is alienated from herself, expropriated and appropriated. Remaining there beside the Mother, she is in fact in motion in a way totally beyond her grasp. She surrenders, she lets it happen; and somehow or other she is aware that, in a manner of speaking, it has nothing to do with her: it is something that takes place in the Lord; yet he permits it to take place in her too.

Magdalen knows little of the Mother. The mysteries of her virginal motherhood are hidden from her, even if she senses in faith that the Incarnation of the Messiah must involve profound miracles. It is not only that she has never observed any sin in Mary; somehow her faith tells her that such a thing would be impossible. An unsurpassable purity has made her worthy of being the Mother of the Lord.

And as Magdalen watches the Mother standing there beneath the Cross, sensing that in some way she is being carried by her—just as she knows that the Son is carrying her, but in a different way—it becomes more and more clear to her that her manner of suffering with the Lord is quite different from his Mother's. The Son dies on the Cross for sinners. And she was the sinner out of whom he drove seven demons. He purified her as it were in anticipation of the fruits of the Cross. It was the Cross that empowered him to drive them out. Her faith had taught her something of this wellspring of grace, and so she lived together with the Lord in prospect of the Cross. And now that it has become actuality, for her it is the key to all that has been. This is the basis on which the Lord drove out her demons; this is what has entitled him to set her among his disciples. On the Cross he is paying for what he has done. And the freedom from sin which he gave her, this freedom for God, was the fruit of what is now taking place before her eyes. Gratefully she accepted his gifts, glad to be rid of sin and able to breathe freely in the air of faith; but now, for the first time, she sees the price of these gifts and understands that, in consenting to what happened then, she has become responsible for what is taking place now. Then, her consent to what was happening to her was only embryonic (for she hardly knew what was happening); now she understands that this first, scarcely definable experience necessarily involved the train of events she is now witnessing. She too was living on credit, and the time had to come—and now it has come—when she herself is summoned.

She is also aware, however, of the great number of sinners who are to be redeemed. She now enters into a new fellowship with them; out of her love for the Lord she wants to belong to them, and it is as though she feels the weight of her long-forgiven sins all over again. The burden of sins borne by the Lord reveals the grievous weight of sin incurred by all sinners, including the weight of Magdalen's own forgiven sin. The Mother, who is without sin, also shares in this fellowship with sinners, precisely because she is the Mother and loves the Son, and because it is partly for love of her that the Son redeems men and, on the Cross, gives them his Mother to be their Mother. His Mother too recognizes in the Son's suffering the precondition for her own preredemption. What would she have been if the Son had not bestowed grace on her in this way? She does not know. But this very "if" now looms large in her soul. In Magdalen we see a visible embodiment of the community of sinners; she accepts responsibility for herself and for all. Thus she is united with the Lord, who accepts responsibility for everything whatsoever. But the Mother is not excluded; she stands in the middle, ineffably, between the two of them. Since Magdalen is now completely pure, what she bears is not only for her own sins; she has been opened up to share in the purity of Mother and Son.

TO THE TOMB

(Mark 15:47–16:1)

Mary Magdalen and Mary the mother of Joses saw where he had been laid. By witnessing the Lord's entombment, the women, without knowing it, are doing something that will expand the Christian faith beyond its pattern hitherto and into a new freedom: not a wanton freedom—for this new liberation is the result of an even closer bond with the Lord, who himself has been laid bound in the grave— but the kind of freedom that is necessary if we are to stand on our own feet in working for the Lord, the freedom that is essential to guarantee the passing on of a mission that is no longer tied to the Lord's earthly presence. Magdalen watches the dead body being put into the tomb, the stone being rolled into place and sealed: a sober, almost brutal fact, which will take its place among the other facts of history. Magdalen must make a note of it, she must make a deliberate effort to remember where the Lord's body lies and how long it has been there.

This fact is the utterly logical result of his whole life
and activity, but all the same it is very puzzling. His
death is very tangibly an end, yet no end was set by
the Lord himself. Magdalen's earthly ministry to the
Lord is past, yet the Lord did not dismiss her from
his service. Until now her faith was wholly linked
to serving the Lord actually present with her, with
his human needs and his actual, verbal instructions.
Thus—assuming that those who followed him were
possessed of living faith—there could be no dispar-
ity between faith and the Lord's teaching. But now
the Lord is dead. He no longer supplies Magdalen
with further material for her faith. As a believer she
is thrown back on herself; she must come to grips
with what she has been given. Since the Lord has
not dismissed her from serving him, she continues
to go with him, beyond the event of his death, to
the grave. She does it automatically, like a maid
who keeps on doing her work even when the master of the house is away. She is aware that something has gone for ever, she knows that when Jesus
is laid in the tomb it is the final resting place of
his earthly path. But since she is still in service she
must feel her way forward, even here at the end,
even at the tomb and—though the tomb must not
be left out—beyond it. What she does not know
is the form that this way forward (or rather, this
leap forward) will take. But at any rate it has to be
found in the Lord's teaching. And his whole life

so far, without exception, belongs to his teaching.
So it is important for Magdalen to have shared his
life, including the entombment, during her time as
a disciple. There is a whole area in this ministry of
witness that is beyond her sight. She performs her
service in a spirit of obedience that she would not
have been able to explain. There is no trace of curi-
osity in her as she watches; she acts out of an inner
necessity that is harmoniously in order and subject
to the Lord.

For the present the Lord's entombment amounts
to the utter end of hope for the women who stand
watching. So long as the body was not yet in the
grave they could hope, somehow or other, that this
death was not real. The suffering had to be gone
through, but since he who was suffering was the
Son of God, it might turn out that he had not died
at all. But what we have now is a thorough demonstration of the genuineness of his death. The body
is wrapped in a winding sheet and left in the tomb
behind a sealed stone. The cloud of hopelessness
that now settles on the women is not a weakness of
faith on their part. It is a burden deliberately placed
on their shoulders: a night that is most closely con-
nected with the night of the Cross, robbing them
not only of the sight of the Lord but of something
much more intimate: it robs them of living in the
medium of his hope, it robs them of the sense of
being able, day by day, to face up to the new tasks

he set them. Yet this same night, and the with-
drawal of his presence that it involves, also form a
constituent part of their faith. Up to now they had
not been aware of it; it is only revealed to them
now that the dead Lord has been made inaccessible to them. They are like abandoned souls who
keep on praying and serving in spite of the fact that
all reason for doing so seems to have disappeared,
and their prayer and service meet with no response.
What they are going through is a very original form
of the Dark Night of the Soul. Remorselessly it
introduces a divorce between the past and future
modes of service; the two modes meet in this night,
they are joined together under cover of its darkness; but those who are enduring the dark night are
aware only of separation. The women's presence at
the entombment, in terms of their observation of an
earthly event, still belongs to the old faith; on the
other hand, seen as the act of a faith that is stronger
than death in spite of the lack of tangible reason for
hope, it has superseded and gone beyond it. This
"going beyond" is of the essence of the fully developed Christian faith.

*And when the sabbath was past, Mary Magdalen and
Mary the mother of James and Salome, bought spices,
so that they might go and anoint him.* The women
pass the sabbath in observing the rest prescribed
by the Law; they also spend it in the darkness of

their separation from the Lord. In temporal terms this "night" stretches from the Lord's death until his resurrection. He descends to hell, to the hopeless realms of death. In the underworld he is cut off from everyone, including the women. In the underworld, preparations are begun for the Lord's Easter Day, and so too preparations are being made for the women's faith. Yet hope remains veiled as this preparation takes place; it is laid up, kept safe in God the Father. "Why" questions—Why this period of waiting? Why this separation? Why does the new need any preparation?—must remain totally unanswered. The journey through the darkness binds all the senses in such a way that the question of a destination does not even arise.

The women are in the Lord's "night"; but at the same time—and this affords some relief—they belong to the Law. It is as though the Sabbath commandment respects their night; as though it exists to protect their present condition, to allow it to run its course, uninterrupted by external issues. There must be no flight from it; nothing must be permitted to awaken in them the least suspicion of new hope and of transformed service. For a while the law of the Sabbath ministers to the New Covenant; it plays a substantial part in preparing the ground, in the women, for their Easter hope and their service to the Easter message. The Law, which keeps them—like the Lord's resting body—immobile for a time, holds them fast on Holy Saturday. The Sabbath as such is good. The Old Covenant is in profound agreement with the New. Since the Old Covenant is oriented to the New, it helps to illuminate the Easter event in its entire fulness.

Then, on Easter Eve, the Law releases the believers so that their faith can undergo its Easter transformation, so that, in this very night, the preparations for Easter can begin. They do not know what is coming, and yet somehow they already experience a certain relief; they take the first preliminary step toward a new life. It must have seemed like a postscript to the old life—they bought spices to anoint the body—but unbeknown to them it led on to the new. They follow their plan and make the appropriate arrangements. The Old Law will not hinder them, but not until the Easter event takes place will they be finally liberated from the Old Covenant and completely made believers in Jesus. Internally, of course, their faith was already a New Testament faith. But it still had a Jewish shell: the new content had not yet fashioned a new form for itself. Love was there, that love which was its whole substance, but the resurrection was needed to help it attain its earthly visible, ecclesial form.

What the women intend to do is the local custom, something they are familiar with and at home with; what they are doing is no different from what other people of their time would have done.

But their aim is to anoint the body of the Son of God. In all reverence they intend to take charge of the Lord's body. However, at the Last Supper the Lord had already disposed of his flesh and blood and given them to everyone. The women have come too late to do what they had in mind. When the Lord was alive, a woman who was a sinner had anointed him while he sat at a meal; she did not know what she had done, but the Lord thanked her by forgiving her sins. Mary of Bethany had anointed him a second time while he was eating at her house; she too did not know the significance of what she had done, and the Lord accepted it as her anointing of his body for burial. But now the redemptive deed to which the anointing referred has been done, and the ancient usages have lost their meaning. Believers no longer need be concerned about making the transition from the Old to the New Covenant: the Lord himself has become the only bridge.

When the Sabbath ran out on Easter Eve, it was also the end of the visible service rendered by the Old Covenant in furtherance of the Lord's purposes. The complete and valid fulfilment has come. Not the limited fulfilment in terms of his Incarnation, his life and suffering, but the fulfilment brought about in his resurrection to eternal life. The bounds of the Old Covenant are fixed here, but the faith of the New Covenant, hand in hand with the Risen Christ,

bursts these bounds. Through the Lord's grace the
precepts of the Old Covenant were kept in force
until Easter Eve to underline the intelligibility of
the New Covenant. Now they must fall silent,
showing that it has superseded them. So the wom-
en's plan can no longer be carried out; instead, it
forms a prelude to the growth of a completely new,
Christian mission. Their intention was a proper
one, yet in its very propriety it was absurd because
the miracle of the resurrection had robbed it of
its object.

THE RISEN LORD

(Matthew 28:1; Mark 16:4; John 20:2, 11–18)

Now after the Sabbath, toward the dawn of the first day of the week, Mary Magdalen and the other Mary went to see the sepulchre. At the earliest possible hour Magdalen goes to the grave. She spent the evening after the Sabbath in buying and preparing the herbs; she cannot rest, thinking of what she is going to do. She does not know what the outcome will be, but she does what is necessary, step by step, without losing any time. The "correct time" is the Lord's time; not to lose time means abiding in his will, even if, in retrospect, doing his will may look like a waste of time.

She goes to look for the tomb. She has a definite aim; she knows the tomb from having stood watching while the Lord was put into it. She is going to anoint the Lord's body, but first she goes to find the tomb. How will it look now, after all that has taken place between Good Friday and Easter morning—events of which she knows nothing? She

47

is not expecting her early morning search to reveal anything. The tomb will not look any different from what it did two days ago. But Magdalen knows that this is something she must do. She would not have been able to give reasons. This shows not only that she is perfectly ready to accept whatever mission she will be given, but that, moreover, she is already performing things that are of the essence of this mission.

Her faith is in a strange state of suspension. On the one hand the Lord is dead; she cannot say she is carrying out his explicit intentions. On the other hand, although she belongs to the Church, she cannot claim, in visiting the tomb, to be carrying out the orders of the apostles, of Peter and John for instance. And yet she must perform this task, which has been given to her personally. She has been inspired to visit and behold the grave, without any clear understanding of the implications. She is simply performing an act of faith, of direct obedience to God; because it lacks all intrinsic evidence, it is expressly the obedience of faith. God can give reasons for the tasks he gives us if he so wishes: thus he can refute the objections of Ananias, sent to visit Saul after his conversion, and illuminate the inner meaning of his particular task. To Magdalen, however, no explanation is given; her experience of life together with the Lord is what guarantees her absolute and unquestioning obedience. It is an entirely human obedience, employed to strengthen her faith and inwardly to empower it to "go beyond". In a way, she goes to the grave blind, in order to receive thence the light of faith.

And looking up, they saw that the stone was rolled back. Magdalen came to look at the closed grave, and what confronts her is an open one—the opposite of what she was expecting. Yet all the same she does see precisely what she came to see. She wanted one thing; the Lord had something else in mind. Doing and expecting the wrong thing, she actually does what the Lord intended. Afterward she will realize that everything was in the right place, but for the moment faith asks too much of her, as her expectations are disappointed and she is faced with something she absolutely cannot comprehend. And in the context of this incomprehension, because she remains obedient and has faith—a faith that has now become inexplicable—she determines to carry out that for which the Lord has brought her here. Her faith embraces and goes beyond everything: that part of her faith which is capable of being disappointed is now totally secondary, because she believes everything the Lord sets before her, even what is unknown and incomprehensible. Her faith faces the Lord so exactly that he can use it and expand it as he wishes, developing it along the lines of his own obedience and trust in his Father. Her faith is lodged securely in the Lord's will; it is a clear expression of his will, the whole extent of which she does not know. All she can say is that his will also embraces her will to see the grave, her finding of the empty tomb. In the Lord's will there is a continuous process; Magdalen only sees individual and apparently unconnected phases, but all the same each stage leads her infallibly to the next. This structure of Catholic faith will become part of the Church. The Christian believes all that the Church proposes for his belief, even if he cannot grasp the whole, even if there are details he cannot understand. For what the Church administers is the Lord's entire revelation, and no believer will ever be able to plumb its depths or envisage its whole compass.

So she ran and went to Simon Peter and the other disciple, the one whom Jesus loved, and said to them, "They have taken the Lord out of the tomb, and we do not know where they have laid him." The fact of the empty tomb is not Magdalen's property; it is part of the process of faith. But this act of faith is universal. She is the one chosen to make it in the first place, but it is not limited to her; she does not keep it to herself. So it is appropriate that she reports it to the two representatives of the Church (representing Church office and love, respectively). She gives her message according to the Lord's will, and it is received by the two apostles who, likewise according to the Lord's will, have been prepared to accept it. In Magdalen, faith is something utterly personal, and so it is in the apostles too. Faith is never a rigid, finished thing but a principle of life, something that upholds and nourishes, out of its abundance, the relationship between the unique individual and the unique Lord. Peter's faith, John's faith are fully in harmony both with their persons and with their task in the Church. But in each case faith's fulness resides in the Lord—where it is both unity and identity—and it is he who freely decides how it shall be transmitted and accepted.

Now Magdalen has come to witness emptiness; later she will be able to testify to fulness. Both must be witnessed to, for both darkness and light are prayer. She must bid farewell to Holy Saturday so that she can truly proclaim Easter. The faith that manifests itself in this twofold witness has its center in the Lord: in the event of his descent to hell and his resurrection. In bearing her testimony Magdalen transcends herself; she is not aware of the full significance of her message, but since she is activated by faith, her faith goes beyond her, it surpasses what she believes and knows.

But Mary stood weeping outside the tomb, and as she wept she stooped to look into the tomb; and she saw two angels in white, sitting where the body of Jesus had lain, one at the head and one at the feet. They said to her, "Woman, why are you weeping?" She said to them, "Because they have taken away my Lord, and I do not know where they have laid him." Saying this, she turned round and saw Jesus standing, but she did not know that it was Jesus. Jesus said to her, "Woman, why are you weeping? Whom do you seek?" Supposing him to be the gardener, she said to him, "Sir, if you have carried him away, tell me where you have laid him, and I will take him away." Jesus said to her, "Mary." She turned and said to him in Hebrew, "Rabboni!" (which means Teacher). Jesus said to her, "Do not hold me, for I have not yet ascended to the Father; but go to my brethren and say to them, I am ascending to my Father and your Father, to my God and your God." Mary Magdalen went and said to the disciples, "I have seen the Lord"; and she told them that he had said these things to her. Mary stands in faith at the empty tomb and sees the two angels. It is because she has faith that she is able to see them. It is a sign of her faith that she sees them, that a conversation is possible between the angels and herself, for conversations with angels are prayers. The attitude of prayer is essential whenever there is to be a genuine dialogue with a heavenly being. Without such an attitude of prayer, Mary would not have been able to speak to the angels.

However, she weeps. Her tears are completely in accord with her human nature, with the earthly part of her faith; they form the watershed between "natural" and "supernatural" faith. In this connection "natural" faith means the faith of those who were acquainted with the Lord during his earthly life. For faith to be faith at all, it has to be open to supernatural faith. Many of those we call unbelievers, who were acquainted with the Lord and impressed by him, accepting his word with a measure of love, came close to having a natural faith of this kind. And for those who "believed in him", who had a genuine "supernatural" faith, the natural relationship was a very significant contributory factor. He was the Master, they the disciples. He was the one who was able to answer their questions. What primarily struck them about him was that he was the perfect man; secondarily, in the background, they were aware of a latent divine mystery. And their "natural" faith was an ever-open door to "supernatural" faith, continually stimulating and animating it. This is a tension that characterizes the faith of later Christians too. "When did we give you to eat and drink, and when did we visit you?" Believers have immediate and natural motives for their deeds of love, motives of which they are conscious; but because they have faith, the Lord is able to expand these motives. He himself enters their actions, with the result that, by way of their fellow men and unbeknown to themselves, what they do involves the God-man; their deeds reach him.

Magdalen weeps tears for the friend she has lost. For her it is a twofold loss: he died on the Cross, and his body has disappeared from the tomb. Thus do her tears demonstrate the border between nature and supernature: this true, supernatural faith, such as the Lord looks for, is not close enough to her, not conscious and discerning enough in her, to hold back her tears.

So it comes about that, when the Lord is actually standing visibly before her, she is so preoccupied by wondering where they have taken him that she cannot recognize him. But she was not meant to recognize him: the words that come forth out of her nonrecognition are very important words for the Church's faith. Again and again her faith manifested a certain poverty of recognition. Here it is stressed once more as she sees the Lord present yet does not know him. We see that the supernatural is stronger in her than nature; her supernatural obedience is more powerful than her ability to know things through the senses. Had she, as a believer, not been so possessed by God, so unreservedly devoted to him, her eyes would have been bound to tell her who was standing before her. But, in the obedience in which she finds herself, her senses have been smitten as though with blindness. It is her faith that blinds her. She believes so firmly that she fails to recognize what she sees. This is what the Lord wills; in her faith she carries out his will.

The Lord speaks to her and in doing so reveals his special fondness for her. He gives himself to her in a way that surpasses her whole nature. In addressing

her, he reveals himself to her supernaturally, for
all the Son's words originate in his eternal dialogue
with the Father and are therefore supernatural.
And with these words he releases her senses, restor-
ing their receptivity. Suddenly, both naturally and
supernaturally at the same time, she realizes that it is
he. The proportions of her faith have been reversed.
Up to now it stood on the basis of nature and tran-
scended itself, becoming supernatural. Now the
supernatural has become the basis; from this vantage
point the natural is comprehended and regained.

"Master!" she cries; and behind this word lies
the perfect union of her two kinds of faith. It also
shows that she has realized what her mission is.
Until now she lived according to a kind of preliminary vocation consisting of an unfathomable faith
and a blind obedience. No limits could be defined
or applied. But in giving her his real presence the
Lord gives her everything that he had previously
kept in suspension. He had to take everything away
from her, because that was the only way he could
teach her what he wanted from her. Now she can
be the bearer of the Easter message of faith. Previously she had gone to the Church with the message of Holy Saturday—the message of emptiness,
of the end, a riddle that resisted all understanding.
Now she proclaims to the Church the fulness of the
Lord's resurrection, the beginning of everything, a
reality grasped and understood. For now all is made

plain: she understands, she knows, she sees. This one word, "Master!" shows that the Lord's plan has been fulfilled in her, that the fulness of the encounter with him has resulted in a fulness in her.

"Do not hold me, for I have not yet ascended to the Father." Here we have the exact converse of the Mother's conception through the Holy Spirit: on that occasion the Mother had to lay hold on the Son in her womb. That is why he came from the Father. But in the meeting with Magdalen his *coming* from the Father has reached an end; this is the turning point: now it is a case of *going* to the Father. She meets him and receives him in a way that is beyond all laying hold. The basis for her mission must be supplied by a faith that can do without sight, the sight that lays hold. The whole mission is a matter of pure faith and needs no further attestation by appearances of the Lord. Magdalen has become confirmed in holiness, just as the Mother was confirmed in holiness at her conception. And whereas the Mother was redeemed in anticipation of the Cross, Magdalen was clearly and tangibly redeemed as a result of the Cross.

THE WOMAN WHO
WAS A SINNER

Hope

(Luke 7:36–50)

PRELUDE

One of the Pharisees asked him to eat with him, and he went into the Pharisee's house and sat at table. A Pharisee invites the Lord, and the latter accepts, for every proper request is welcome to him. Having become man, he hears men's pleas in a human manner and responds. And his responding is part of the total context of his great promise: "If you ask the Father anything in my name, he will give it to you." By responding to them as a man he will help them to understand that God too responds. The Son became man in order to train men to do the Father's will, to present his will to them in such a way that they can understand it and correspond to it. If he responds to their human requests, they will be inclined to believe that the Father, in turn, will fulfil the Son's requests, and thus that he will also fulfil their requests if they are brought before him by the Son. In fulfilling human requests the incarnate Son becomes a manifestation of divine fulfilment by the Father.

At the same time, however, the Son shows the Father how seriously he regards this communication of his fatherly will, how much he is involved with it, how diligent he is in carrying out the Father's commission. In acceding to the Pharisee's request he is also responding to a request from the Father. The Father, whose will the Son does, desires him to visit the Pharisee, not only so that the human response may manifest something of the divine, but so that he may use this opportunity, together with the Son, to proclaim a new truth to men: the truth of hope. A new form of hope is to be given them, arising out of the Lord's meeting with the woman who was a sinner. This one example will show men what kind of hope they can place in the Redeemer. This unique encounter will be incorporated into the permanent structure of both penance and Eucharist; it contains, in germ, the entire redemptive hope in which Christians of all times will approach the Lord in these sacraments.

So Jesus enters the house to which he has been invited and sits down at table. He does this simple thing in the same way that he does everything in life, within the perspective of his Father's will and of his own will as Redeemer, in order to reveal a new aspect of his Father's truth and his own truth. The Pharisee's house is a house like any other; yet, like every house, it is different from all others. But however that may be, the presence of the Son makes it into a house of the Father, a place of truth, a place of the Word—the Word that the Son is, but also the Word that the Son proclaims, revealing the meaning of the triune God in a way that is eternally new. What is new this time is hope. Commissioned by the Father and in collaboration with the Holy Spirit, the Son is here to do for the woman who was a sinner what he wants to do for every sinner; he wants to awaken a hope and make it a reality.

Behold, a woman of the city who was a sinner.... The Son came into the world because we are all sinners. The very fact that we were born in original sin makes us all sinners in the sight of the Father. Then there is the fact of the sins we personally commit. There is not one of us who, in the presence of the Lord, should feel that he is not a sinner. However, he came to rescue all sinners. And as far as our sins are concerned, up to a certain point we know what they are, but only God knows the full truth about them. Also, as regards our fellow man, we may know that he is a sinner, but we cannot assess the number and gravity of his sins.

As we have here a parable of hope, the woman who is to meet the Lord is called a sinner more explicitly than others. Sin must cling to her externally as well, so that everyone can understand the role she plays opposite the Lord. She lives in sin and by sin. This sin is not only known to her: everyone else knows of it too. She is a sinner so unequivocally that the epithet suffices to designate her; it would never occur to anyone to ask to what extent she is aware or perhaps unaware of her sin, what excuses might be made for her or how far she is herself responsible or has been driven to it by others. She is simply "the sinner". Perhaps the only thing that makes her different from us is that her trade and her reputation proclaim what she is outwardly. For her, her existence and her sin form a unity, for she lives as a sinner. But all of us can see ourselves in her; our sins may be less public, less clearly defined, but none of us can say we have nothing in common with her. We are all sinners. So, all of a sudden, it is as if this woman of the city who was a sinner includes each of us, as if she encounters the Lord in the name of all those who are destined to come to know hope. All who are to be redeemed are to behold in her the power of divine grace; for the sake of all, the Lord uses this particular woman who sums up in herself our manifold need of redemption. Who was more in need of redemption than this notorious sinner! And could there be a more exciting and impressive encounter than this one, between the woman who was a sinner and him who embodied the grace of the Father!

THE PHARISEE AND THE SINNER

... when she learned that he was sitting at table in the Pharisee's house, she brought an alabaster flask of ointment. ... She knows about the Lord, but in a way that, previously, did not involve her. An abyss yawned between them: he was the Lord, she the sinner; what could they possibly have in common? She presumes that he knows what everyone else in the town knows: he is bound to know that she is a sinner. But what she does not know is that he knows about her as one for whose sake he became man; that in his eyes she is the sinner for whom he is willing to die; that she is one of the many, and yet at the same time she is the one person, the only person on whom he has put all his hope (and for him hope means awaiting the Father's good pleasure, waiting for the fulfilment of the Father's plan). She does not know that, in his eyes, she incarnates all sinners in herself, nor that he finds her incarnate in all the others. She does not know that he will find in her a confirmation of his vocation. She is not aware that she is entering into a relationship with his unique hope that through her will fulfil and perfect it.

She does know that he is something special. According to what she has heard about him, he seems like a representative of God, for a while dwelling among men. And this hearsay awakens hope within her. But this hope is only a preparation for what actually takes place. She gets herself ready, and in the same sense she prepares the vessel of ointment. She gets ready to go to him, and in so doing she is saying her Yes to him. However, it is not she who molds this Yes: she will receive it from him in the very act of anointing him. She goes to him in the way we go to God in faith, putting all our hope in him, but at the same time making room for him, the room he needs if he is to dwell in us. The very fact that she goes is a sign of her readiness; the latter is so great that the encounter with the Lord will fulfil her hopes: she will do what the Lord expects of her. On her side her hope will be fulfilled in him, but even as hope it is so great that she leaves all fulfilment up to him. In going to him she is performing a great self-emptying. She gets the flask ready too. Just as she prepares herself, bursting with hope, she prepares the flask, filling it with the ointment, so that both she and the flask are completely filled at this meeting. She may have filled the flask without in the least realizing why. Or if she did know why, it was a very imperfect knowledge. She may have thought of anointing him in some way, but prior to encountering him she cannot know that she is going to anoint *Christ* with the anointing he both expects and needs.

Viewed externally, her act of going to the Lord is still a part of her sinful life, a part of *her* life. Initially it looks like a compromise gesture, although it already contains elements of purity and is free of any sinful intention. And perhaps, in the course of her sinful life, she has approached many a man hoping in some way or other for release, obscurely aware that some day things must be different. But somehow she also knows that this "some day" is not something she can bring about; it is something she must leave to the other person. Perhaps, then, this hope has been alive within her, in a vague way, for a long time; perhaps she actually sees the ointment intended for the Lord as the objective symbol of her hope—her hope in tangible form. In this case the ointment would indicate that this occasion is different from all the others. The fact that she takes the ointment with her shows the difference between her approach to the Lord and ours, most of the time. While we do approach him with an indefinite kind of hope, it is vitiated by a "perhaps" that is pitifully short of genuine hope. We fail to contribute what we can to bring our hope into accord with what the Lord hopes. Thus it is far harder for the Lord to transform our "perhaps" into certainty than to bring certainty to this sinful woman.

Though she is a sinner, she does not want to come to the Lord empty handed. Her alabaster flask with the ointment symbolizes all the ways in which men prepare for Christianity. It is an image of human merit as opposed to grace; it is like the bag of belongings, containing all that he has, that a man carries over his shoulder as he makes his way toward salvation. It is like the confession into which he puts all his sins, like a funeral pyre awaiting only the flame, like a boundless hope, much too great to be fulfilled, too immense to dare believe in. And yet the time has come to live for this hope, to cultivate it and take great care lest it be quenched. A line is drawn, bringing what has been to a close.

The alabaster flask is the form of the past. What it contains is the promise of the Old Covenant. What has this woman got to do with the Old Covenant? Much, surely: What would she be without the past? The vessel, the nard, the woman: they seem to be unrelated; taken in isolation they have nothing in common. But they have been drawn into a movement, a movement of hope in the Lord, fitted together into a unity according to the laws and requirements of hope.

... and standing behind him at his feet, weeping, she began to wet his feet with her tears and wiped them with the hair of her head and kissed his feet and anointed them with the ointment. There is nothing here about the

Lord, about how he looks, how he reacts. All the light falls on the woman and her behavior. She is the one he has been waiting for, and now there she is, as large as life. Two hopes have become one: hers and his. Her hope casts itself at the Lord's feet; what we see is not a radiant hope but a weeping woman. And every tear is a revelation that deeply moves the Lord; each tear is a word with which she unveils her life, speaking more plainly and accurately than words can; these silent tears tell everything that cannot be told.

They flow so freely that the Lord's feet are, as it were, bathed in tears. The Lord is touched by these confessed sins; he feels them and experiences them under the form of the woman's contrition which so bodily, visibly and tangibly pours from her. But, once having begun, she is determined to perform her task properly: having wet his feet with what is hers, she will also dry them with what is hers— her hair. Simultaneously she wets them and dries them. She both confesses and tries to wipe away the traces that her confession has left on the Lord—as if she is aware how eloquent her tears are; as if she knows that they bespeak many sins and is reluctant to burden the Lord with them; as if it would be too much to hope that her sins could really be taken over by the Lord; as if she ought not to presume that he will take her tears and let them flow through him to God; as if there are limits, in hope, beyond

which one cannot go. She does not penetrate the
mystery to which she is ministering. All she knows
is that she still has to anoint him, and so his feet
must be dried. But since this anointing is in a way
a preparation for the Cross, she herself must not
preempt the Cross; all she can do is confirm the
need for it, showing how much she needs to be
redeemed, recounting the extent of her sins. Even-
tually she comes up against the limit; she can no
longer give her hope any definite shape; she has to
extinguish it as *her* hope and let it be sublimated in
the Lord's will and purpose.

The encounter between them is introduced
by an invisible little ceremony: the woman takes
a definite number of steps toward him. It would
be importunate, indiscreet to go further, but she
may and must go so far. She must approach until
she comes to the edge of that sphere which is the
Lord's alone. She falls down; she worships and confesses; but her prayer and her confession go no further than the Lord's threshold. She must cease what
she has been doing, she must wipe it away, lest she
seem to be putting the Lord under an obligation.
And she uses her own hair to wipe away her tears.
Suddenly it is as if she has performed a kind of *man-
datum,* feet washing; as if she has tested the Lord's
approach in confession, acting as an instrument
in the Father's hand, demonstrating to him once
more the Son's perfection, showing how firmly he

stands at the center of the Father's will and does not presume to take anything upon himself. His own instrumentality is illuminated in a new way by the woman's. His hour is coming, but it is not here yet. The woman's task is to draw the sharp outline of this coming hour.

Now when the Pharisee who had invited him saw it, he said to himself: If this man were a prophet, he would have known who and what sort of woman this is who is touching him, for she is a sinner. The Pharisee's relation to the Lord is a strange one. He is looking for something from him, otherwise he would not have invited him, but he is not sure what. Rumor has brought many things to his ears about the Lord, but nothing that demands inner commitment from him. In his eyes the Lord is simply a celebrity, a man from whom he can learn much that is interesting and stimulating. But it would never occur to him to feel that the Lord had any claim on him; he would not dream of making any kind of revelation to him or of resisting him inwardly. No doubt the Lord belongs to a certain class of people; it is just that, for the moment, the Pharisee is not quite sure how to classify him. He has heard about the miracles, but they do not convince him. He knows that, as Son of God, the Lord has a particular relationship to the heavenly Father, but it does not seem to him to be an explicitly divine relationship. As for himself, he believes that there is a God in heaven. He knows of the ancient promises, of the prophets of the Old Covenant, of the coming Messiah. He knows that the Messiah will have a special mission, like that of the prophets. But he is cautious. He calculates. We hear him calculating as he says to himself: If this man were a prophet, he would have known.... He thinks that prophets are equipped with a kind of supernatural sixth sense that enables them to distinguish spirits. If the Lord had such a gift, he would have started back in horror at the first touch. For to the Pharisee nothing is more revolting than sin. He hates sin. But, more than sin itself, he hates it being made public, laid bare, coming to the surface. A hidden, disguised sin is far less grievous to him than a sin that has been made public. He endeavors to keep sin as far from himself as possible; but he is even more assiduous in avoiding contact with sinners, lest he be tarred with the same brush. The respect of his fellow men means a great deal to him. And he sees the Lord in the same terms. If he were a prophet, he would have nothing in common with sinners, not only because he himself would not be a sinner, but even more because he would avoid every occasion of coming into contact with a sinner. The unbeliever cannot grasp the fact that, as the incarnate Son of God, the Lord seeks contact with sin, that he has actually come looking for sin, that he loves to be with sinners because he loves men, who are sinners, and wants to redeem them. As far as the Pharisee is concerned there is no relation whatsoever between the Lord's mission and the life of this sinful woman. According to the Pharisee, if the Lord were a prophet he would distinguish clearly in this case; his judgment would yield a decision, the only decision possible to a Pharisee: avoid all contact. One thing is certain, then: this man is no prophet. Such a verdict does not mean that, in the Pharisee's eyes, the Lord is just an ordinary man like anyone else; he is still a special, unusual and interesting person whom it is worth getting to know. But he is not a prophet. The Pharisee is the embodiment of a fixed faith that is incapable, for the time being, of expansion; a faith that, in spite of God's warning against judging others, is always doing just that. It is always judging according to its own standards, its own truth, its own self-imposed restrictions, which spell the death of faith. Faith can only live if it is continually expanding and encompassing more and more territory. But in the Pharisee's case the whole terrain has already been parceled out. Judgment has already been passed: the Lord's contact with the sinner plainly indicates his lack of supernatural knowledge.

THE PARABLE

And Jesus answering said to him, "Simon, I have some-
thing to say to you." And he answered, "What is it,
Teacher?" ... "A certain creditor had two debtors; one
owed five hundred denarii, and the other fifty. When
they could not pay, he forgave them both. Now which of
them will love him more?" Simon answered, "The one,
I suppose, to whom he forgave more." And he said to
him, "You have judged rightly." The Lord turns to
the Pharisee. He has something to tell him—to tell
him and no one else. He has a personal message
for him, applying to him in the most personal way
in his present situation. The one and only Lord has
one particular thing to say to this particular Pharisee. Making parables is something the Lord likes
to do, but he never does so arbitrarily, because
the Son's inventiveness resides in the Father. And
God's inventiveness is always, among other things, a
response to the questions that mankind puts to him,
a response adapted to men's requests and designed
to render the love of God intelligible to them. The
"something" that the Lord has to say to Simon is
therefore something meant to reveal his love for

men. He does this by giving an instance. It applies particularly to the Pharisee; it is something he will understand; but it so pulsates with truth, eternal and entire, that not only this Pharisee, but all Pharisees, and not only this man, but the whole of humanity, will be able to grasp the truth of it, in every possible sense, literal and metaphorical. The Now gives birth to the Eternal; this particular, applied truth yields all truth. This word addressed to the Pharisee becomes the Word who is Jesus.

The Pharisee replies, "What is it, Teacher?" We can detect here, faintly, how he is beginning to retract what he had said to himself earlier. He recognizes the Teacher again. He has refused to grant him the title of prophet, but, confronted by the Lord, he is so moved that he simply has to call him Teacher. It is as if what the Lord says reestablishes him in the right relationship to him. The very fact that the Pharisee is no longer thinking his own thoughts, but is ready to hear what the Lord has to say, shows that the relationship between them has been put on a proper footing. His readiness is contained within the offer being made to him; his response of service takes place in the context of grace; he senses an inner compulsion, but it flows from his free-will desire to hear what the Lord has to say. This desire itself implies a certain awareness of the grace of the Lord, an expectation, even an initial adumbration of a hope.

So the Lord starts to tell his parable: There was a certain creditor. For the moment he is simply that and nothing else: a creditor. The Lord himself is this creditor, and we are all in debt to him. Our entire relationship to him can be reduced to this one thing: we have debts owing to him. Through all eternity he is making demands of us, and rightly so, since we are eternally slow to pay, in arrears, in debt. And now it is as if the Lord is about to reveal the whole fulness of truth all at once, concentrating everything into the parable's succinct words. He limits the debtors to two. One owes a great deal, the other little; but both are debtors, and all the other debtors in the world, all those who owe the Lord anything, can be allotted their place somewhere in this spectrum. But these two, symbolizing all men, have their entire debts—much in the one case and little in the other—forgiven. The creditor makes no distinction. They are both no longer debtors. He decides not to pursue his rightful demands. The slate is wiped clean. They are no longer in debt: they are redeemed. One had felt a heavy burden, the other a light one; but both were lifted by the only person able to do so.

For the sake of the Pharisee the Lord has emphasized the difference between the large and small amounts owing. This was meant to make him reflect on his own debts. In the eyes of God, the creditor to whom the whole world owes everything, there is no difference between large and small. Similarly, for the debtor who is really aware of what he owes to God, there can be no measuring of debts. But the Pharisee is accustomed to measuring things, and the Lord addresses him in these terms to bring him closer to a realm beyond all measurement.

Both debtors had their burden lifted: one would have thought that they would be equally grateful. Yet the Lord asks: Which of them will love their generous lord more? The answer follows naturally: the one whom he forgave more. The parable wastes no words in discussing how hard the debtors would have found it to pay the required sum and how much time it would have taken. The two things are just starkly contrasted: debt and remission. But there is also the contrast between the heavy debt and the light debt, which indicates that the one debtor must have found things extremely difficult, whereas the other might have somehow managed to get by. The former is bound to have been more grateful: previously in desperation, now he can breathe freely again; he can walk with his head up and look to the future and to freedom. Here the Lord has the Pharisee exactly where he wants him: his own system of values, as a Pharisee, must give him some inkling of the greater love that springs from greater mercy, a love built entirely on the unfathomable mercy of God that, beyond all measuring, eliminates the whole measure of debt and guilt.

By taking this path with the Pharisee, the Lord
reveals to him that he can read the heart. He knows
about guilt, great and small. He sees it in the soul
of the woman, who occasioned the content of this
parable. He also sees it in the Pharisee, for whose
sake he gave the parable this particular shape. The
form of the story mirrors the Pharisee's sinful condition. The Lord knows everything; the fact that
he is concerned for the woman does not stop him
from seeing the Pharisee as well and following what
transpires within him.

And hope is there, too, in the middle of it all.
There is hope in the Pharisee. He starts to bury his
initial hope and says: No, this man is no prophet!
But his hope flares up again when the Lord turns his
attention to him, calling him by name and speaking
to him in a personal way. Now his hope is no longer exclusively bound up with his secret thoughts:
it acquires a new shape as the Lord gives it a new
impetus and a change of direction. The focus of
hope is transferred from the listening Pharisee to the
parable itself. For now it is the two debtors who are
important: they no longer dared to hope—this is
not mentioned, but it is implied in the fact that they
could not pay—and suddenly, against all hope, they
are free. At the very moment when they had given
up, everything is given them, an "everything" that
puts an end to all calculation. So, ultimately, hope
resides in the Lord; he produced the parable, and

it is he who stands, full of hope, between the two sinners, the great and the small. Not only does the creditor fulfil the debtors' failing hopes, he also fulfils his own hope by using this unexpected course of action to achieve a just, meaningful and fruitful result. Nothing forces him to act thus; his action flows from the fulness of his free grace. But this creditor is God himself, come among men to release them from their guilt. At this moment, the IOU's he holds in his hand are the sinners' confessions that publicly acknowledge the fact. And in that this state of affairs is wiped away by grace, God's hope is fulfilled—and it is God's fulfilled hope that underlies the hope that springs to life again in the debtor.

Hope is like a light suffusing the whole parable; it is unexpressed and yet fulfilled. It is fulfilled before anyone has time really to notice it. Both the great hope and the small hope are utterly unlikely, but the creditor makes them come true. In sovereign freedom he creates this fulfilment and sets his seal on it. Thus he becomes the one who fulfils every hope, from the smallest to the greatest.

Then turning toward the woman he said to Simon, "Do you see this woman? I entered your house, you gave me no water for my feet, but she has wet my feet with her tears and wiped them with her hair. You gave me no kiss, but from the time I came in she has not ceased to kiss my feet. You did not anoint my head with oil,

but she has anointed my feet with ointment." Everyone had been absorbed in listening to the parable.
It was part of their conversation at table. Perhaps
(the Pharisee may have thought) the Lord was tell-
ing the parable to turn people's attention away from
the woman. And then something happens that neither the Lord's table companions nor the woman
expects: the Lord establishes a connection between
the woman and his host. He addresses Simon at the
same time that he turns to the woman. She is lying
at his feet on the floor, and everything about her
bespeaks the fact that she is a sinner and knows it;
she wants to express her sinfulness in some way. It
is her awareness of sin that has driven her to the
Lord, showing her the infinite abyss that separates
her from him and making her throw herself down
at his feet. Kneeling, lying prostrate, in the attitude
of humility, of abject humiliation, she reveals both
who she is and who he is.

And now the Lord points to her; but he does not
mention what is on her mind, namely, her distance
from him, but something far more important to him
at the moment: the distance between her and the
Pharisee. The Pharisee was well aware of this distance, but, the way he saw it, he was the righteous
one, and she was the sinner; he was the Lord's bona
fide host, whereas she was a gate crasher; she had
come in uninvited and, on account of her sinfulness, would never have been invited in any case.

He looks down on her. The Lord lets the distance between them stand, but he assesses it totally differently. Point by point he shows that the Pharisee is the inferior one, the woman superior: the Pharisee is aloof, uninvolved, unaware and inactive; the woman, by contrast, knows, realizes, acts and responds to the Lord's every wish. She actually fills him with new hope. She goes beyond the Lord's expectations; for as far as his expectations were concerned, they applied to the Pharisee, who disappointed them.

I entered your house. . . . In entering this house the Lord was animated by an unexpressed hope that the Pharisee neither sensed nor fulfilled. Of course he behaved correctly toward the Lord; there is no evidence to suggest that he invited the Lord in order to humiliate him. But he did not understand the implications of this visit, from the Lord's point of view. The Lord did not enter the house of the woman who was a sinner; evidently it was the Pharisee's house on which he set his hopes. Here there is water, but not for washing his feet; oil, but not for anointing him. His host has been remiss: he did not even consider that customs such as these might be meaningful—let alone the question of the kiss. Now, however, lost opportunities will be made good. The woman has neither water nor a towel, yet her repentant love provides her with both: so

that she can wash his feet she is given the gift of
tears; her natural adornment, her hair, seems good
enough for drying his feet. She who thought she
had nothing to bring but her guilt in fact possesses
everything she needs to satisfy the Lord's hope. She
has performed the ablution the Lord expected; not
easily, as the Pharisee might have done, but in the
hardest way: by confessing her guilt, handing over
everything and keeping nothing back, giving the
Lord what seems impossible because he needs it.
She would never dream of being able to satisfy the
Lord's expectations; what she gives, she gives in her
own small way. But all of a sudden it bursts through
and exceeds the expectations not only of the Pharisee but of the Lord as well—his expectations of
what he had expected, here and now, of this sinner.
Suddenly she is the one who is prodigally spending
herself on him, before ever he had visibly poured
out himself for her. She is possessed by his grace.
This very grace empowers her to hasten to meet it;
she actually overtakes his grace, "going beyond" it
in a way that, otherwise, is reserved for God alone.
And what she does is done not only for her but
for the Lord, giving him an opportunity to show
the Pharisee how he should have acted. So her
action has developed beyond the level of repara-
tion for her personal sins to become the Church's
common property. Her contrition, her repentance,
her courage of faith, her hope that soars above all

hesitation, her love that looks only to the Lord: all this, adopted and transformed by the Lord's grace, is made an effective vehicle for his message; it actually becomes part of his good news and his redemptive activity.

The Pharisee did not dare to offer the Lord the kiss of welcome, the kiss of peace and joy. He called him "Teacher", but he did not kiss him. Had he done so, he would not have "said to himself" the things he did. The sinner's kiss of surrender shows that she is not interested in saying anything "to herself". She only wants to do what the Lord wishes. She keeps on kissing his feet, humiliating herself totally, showing that she is nothing; that, in fact, she is not. Thus it is clear that she has been completely absorbed into pure service; she has become pure instrument. Her cooperation in no way hinders the Lord; she desires only to do what he expects without the least reservation. The Pharisee refused to give the one kiss; she supplies kisses beyond number.

Nor did the Pharisee anoint the Lord's head. He made not the slightest move in this direction or in any other. He invited the Lord in order to see what the latter might have to offer him and got stuck in a kind of suspicious anticipation. He kept aloof. It was up to the Lord to produce an outline of his personality; the Pharisee stayed colorless, neutral. This stranger was in his house more to be observed than to be loved. The woman, on the other hand, anointed the Lord's feet. She would not have dared to anoint his head. In her humility she clung to the most lowly part of him. She knew well that, in fact, there was nothing lowly about him, but she chose his feet because this action somehow matched what was lowliest in her. She wanted to keep in the background as far as possible. What she had to do could be done to the Lord's lowest extremities, so that she would not obstruct his higher parts. He must not be restricted, must keep his freedom intact. Moreover, she wanted to stay in the attitude of worship. Her love is of such a kind that it is one with her sorrow for sin; for her, loving is enough. Not until the Lord turns to her in love does she acquire hope.

Therefore I tell you, her sins, which are many, are forgiven, for she loved much; but he who is forgiven little loves little. The Pharisee has condemned the woman. He has condemned her on the basis of her reputation, on the basis of a norm of morality, of behavior, that he finds somewhere within himself. In this scheme of things the concept of love occupies a small and diminishing place; for him it has so shrunk—and he has devoted less and less attention to it—that in the end it has disappeared from his purview entirely. Love lives in the Lord. Love is the reason for his coming, and it is out of love that he will redeem all who are to be redeemed. Love causes him to seek

out and visit every area that is to be redeemed; it is
as if he needs always to be living in the midst of it in
order to love. In the end, for him, love is the only
issue. And this is the very thing for which he looks
in vain in the Pharisee. Since the Pharisee has no
love, he has no proper way of approaching the Lord
and cannot call him by his name, Christ.

Now, however, the Lord applies the criterion of
love to what has been taking place. Earlier, in the
case of the creditor, there was still the question of
calculating amounts. The debts were liquidated, but
it was a case of how much: a lot or a little. And
love depended on the amount of the debt remitted.
But now there is no place for calculation: love is
the criterion, for it is love that allows forgiveness to
take place. The Lord forgives out of love. But love
looks for love in return. Previously the measure of
love encountered was proportional to the debt that
had been forgiven; somehow or other it was calcu-
lable. Now all measurement ceases to apply: love is
immeasurable, it is the prime factor, and forgiveness follows it. Where there is much love, there is
much forgiveness; the woman is different from the
Pharisee, not only in that she has sinned and he has
not, but in that she has loved much, and he has not.
Now all calculations have been wiped out. There is
still a giving and taking, a reciprocal movement, but
it all takes place within love. The Lord is, as it were,
all the more committed, the more love he meets.

This sinful woman, because she loves, makes it easy for him to forgive.

Prior to this, of course, she also lived according to a kind of love, but it was a love that did not stop her sinning, that was not stronger than her will to sin. It was a love that blindly stumbled along, a love that kept hoping. Whatever was pure in her was probably more in the nature of hope than of love. Now that she has met the Lord, has washed his feet with her tears and dried them with her hair, now that she stands in the presence of his love, she has become a genuine lover for the first time. To such an extent that the Lord honors her, he will not expose her as the one who has been relieved of a great burden of debt on the basis of the one-sided operation of grace; on the contrary, he takes her part, he portrays their encounter as a two-sided process in which love hurries to meet love. He praises and stresses the meritorious element of the woman's love. She loves, surrenders herself to love and discovers the love of God. And since the Lord's love is redemption, she is not loved merely in the way she might have expected in view of her particular sin; she is redeemed far beyond the measure of her hopes. She experiences the measure of Christian hope at the moment when it is fulfilled in her.

FORGIVENESS

And he said to her: Your sins are forgiven. Now the
Lord is no longer talking to the Pharisee but to
the woman. He listens and hears words that apply
to her, not to him. He witnesses the fulfilment of the
message of hope. Her sins are forgiven. In speaking
to her the Lord does not mention the word love.
To the Pharisee he explained the interplay of love
given and received, and the woman provided the
illustration. But when he speaks to her, he speaks
of sin. It is just like an ordinary confession in the
church, where it is the absolution that lights up the
whole process; all the other elements—contrition,
the confession of sins, the penance—remain in dim
outline, in a twilight, because really it is the Lord
alone who is at work. And there can be no question of the light of grace somehow beautifying sins
and making them more pardonable. The sins that
are forgiven are *these* sins, real, naked and totally
unforgivable. At this moment the woman knows
more surely than ever that, if she were to look only
at her sins, she would despair. There would not be
the least room left in her for hope. But at the very

point where all she can see is her sin, where she can no longer explain her actions or make excuses for them, where she no longer tries to understand them and has given up trying to pin her hopes on any remaining good quality she might have—at this very point she finds the Lord, forgiving her every-thing. In her there is sin; there is no basis for hope. All hope lies in the meeting with the other, the Lord. Her all-embracing sin meets his all-embracing forgiveness. It is the encounter, serious, sober and effective, between the Lord's love and the sinner's sin. The woman does not come to him as one who, after all, has loved; not as someone who is concen-trating on her better self, not as someone who, after years of blindness, has finally seen the light nor even as someone asking the Lord for grace. She stands before him as one who has sinned and whose sins have been forgiven.

Then those who were at table with him began to say among themselves, "Who is this, who even forgives sins?" The question the Pharisee had asked himself earlier is now put in a wider form. Then it was a case of whether the Lord could have suffered being touched by this woman if he were a prophet. By now his fellow guests have got far beyond seeing him as a prophet: they have come in contact with the Lord's sovereign power. He forgives sins—sins, moreover, which, seen from the outside, are no concern of his. It is not simply a question of forgiving sins done against us, of which the Our Father speaks. It is something quite different. The woman has not sinned against him personally, as a man; humanly speaking, he has nothing to forgive her for. But in fact he forgives these very sins which, humanly speaking, do not refer to him. Who can he be, to feel so affected by other people's sins that he forgives them? And where does he get the power to deal with these sins? One has to be injured or insulted before one can forgive, and the Lord has never seen this woman before!

The answer to their questions lies in the uncharted region between sin and grace, between injury and forgiveness, despair and hope. All ideas about him being a prophet have vanished: a prophet cannot forgive sins. But this man has the gift of forgiveness, the gift of love; and suddenly each of the guests wonders whether he is not one of the two debtors in the parable and this stranger in their midst the creditor, a creditor who has such power that he can even wipe out other people's debts.

And he said to the woman, "Your faith has saved you; go in peace." The Lord is not interested in the other guests' thoughts. At present he is concerned for this believing woman. He is totally absorbed in his work of love. The others' tentative ideas, their reservations, hesitations, refusals and occasional flickerings of hope—for the present they are not his business. "Your faith has saved you."

The woman had found out that he was here. She had come to him, to the Lord in person. She surrendered to him as a guilty, repentant woman, willing to reveal all. She wanted to sacrifice everything for him: material goods, in buying the ointment, and the substantial inner goods represented by her tears; she lent him her hair, she tried to do everything the others had not done. The Lord recognizes all this as her faith. Perhaps initially it was a feeble hope set within a growing love. But the Lord recognizes it as genuine, as belonging to his Father's truth, originating in that eternal coinherence that unites the Son with the Father and the Spirit. Just as the divine Persons belong to one another in eternal life, in a perfectly reciprocal knowledge, so now this woman, through her love for the Lord, also belongs. This love is her living faith, a faith that saves, a faith that both redeems her and helps the others on the way to knowledge. It is a faith that elicits the Lord's final "Go in peace"—a peace composed of faith, love and hope, a peace that is his own peace, that he possesses in order to give to those he redeems. With these words he sends her out into her new life. Henceforth Jesus' hope will go with her. A redeemed woman, she has experienced the fulfilment of his hope, and this hope promises and guarantees the continuance of her encounter with him.

MARY OF BETHANY

Love

"...AND LISTENED TO HIS TEACHING"

THE ONE THING NECESSARY

(Luke 10:38–42)

Now as they went on their way, he entered a village; and a woman named Martha received him into her house. The Lord journeys on his way, animated by his love for the Father. For the incarnate Son there is a threefold aspect to the Father's love for the Son, the Son's love for the Father and the love of both, in the Spirit, for the Spirit. First, they "do everything" in love. This applies right across the board, and no conditions can be laid down for it. It is something that can be observed in each particular act, but such acts do not exhaust it, and hence they cannot be added together to produce a sum total—they express the being of the whole, which is always "beyond"; it is of the essence of these acts that they manifest themselves as belonging to the whole. As it becomes visible, each deed and part points to that which remains invisible in its infinite magnitude.

Then there is the love of Jesus for men, that unmistakable and unique love that is revealed again and again in his many encounters and conversations, in his giving of the commandment of love, in his preaching, in his instructing of the disciples, in his contacts with strangers and those whose names we do not know. And if the first mode of love always pointed back to the Father and the triune mystery, the second, always and without the least diminution, indicates the Son's love for men.

But there is still the third mode, that of love simply in itself. We can think of God as its object, or men, and perhaps we can even think of it without any object at all, love as the source, love pure and simple, love both in becoming and in being, love both in readiness and in performance, love simply for the sake of love, love as a condition of life, love as air, as light.

This love becomes visible as we behold the Lord on his journeys. He proceeds, moves forward, and in an instant this motion sums up his whole life, the meaning of his existence. For the moment we are not concerned with the fact that, over and above this, he prays; nor that he has a particular human destination in view. But in reality this love is never cut off, neither from the Father nor from men; it is pure movement toward both. Even the most jejune details in the Gospel, such as, the Lord "went on his way", he "came" to such-and-such a place, he "stood", are permeated with this love. It is love pure and simple, so much so that it is always approaching

the Father and men; but equally it is always radiating
from the Father and the Spirit, because love's source
is the triune life of heaven, and what becomes a
wellspring in the Son has been welling up in him
from all eternity.

As we contemplate the Lord on his journey, it
is axiomatic that love inspires his steps. He comes
from the Father and goes to the Father, and all the
time he is in the Father. On his way he meets a
woman, and she too does something out of love:
she takes him into her house. This woman is like
the root of a tree, and her sister is the fruit. She
too is part of love, visible love, but in a preparatory
manner: by giving hospitality to the Lord she introduces him to the invisible love with which her sister
contemplates him. Almost without her realizing it,
her active love is in the service of contemplative
love. In fact, she will take offence at this, giving the
Lord the opportunity of speaking about the contemplative love that has its origin in him.

Here again there are three aspects to love: the
Lord on his journey, Martha's activity, and in
the background, shining through her, the tranquil
being of Martha's sister. This contemplative "being"
on the part of Mary of Bethany will turn out to
be the highest response that human love can make
to the Lord. But this love would be impossible unless
it drew its life from the Lord himself; nor could it
issue in any expression without the mediation of

Martha's activity, which brought her and the Lord
together. The fact that Mary's love radiates forth
is a consequence of Martha's action in bringing
the Lord into their house. Martha's action may be
totally eclipsed by the brilliance of what follows
upon it, but all the same it was the precondition for
all that took place. It was the precondition for the
Lord's coming; for the Lord's eternal Advent.

*And she had a sister called Mary, who sat at the Lord's
feet and listened to his teaching.* It is the most natural
thing in the world for Mary to sit at the Lord's feet.
It is the first thing we hear of her, her introduction,
her distinguishing mark. It is her character, her tem-
perament. She sits at his feet, just as, in succeeding
ages, all forms of contemplative life in the Church
will sit at his feet: in order to look up to him—not
to see him one-sidedly, but to be in the right place
for listening to his word. He himself is the Word:
he not only corresponds to it, he is identical with it.
What Mary does is a response to this fact: she wants
to make room for this fact with her whole being.
She not only wants to hear the word; by listening
she wants to receive the Lord into herself, she wants
to be his vessel. Martha received him into her house
externally. Mary receives him into the house of her
own self. This space is free and available within
her because her love makes it so and because she herself is drawn into it. And since it is there exclusively

to receive the Lord, it is perfectly natural for her to sit down at his feet.

It is equally natural for the Lord to begin to speak. It is his response to the conditions he has created. He takes possession of the space he has prepared. And if, while he was journeying from place to place, love was like an invisible ray of light that, constantly in motion, struck no surface, now, suddenly, it shines out brilliantly, having encountered a listener who can receive it. If the love that pours from him is to become visible, it needs the answering love of the one who receives him. This love, which is continually nourished and is continually growing as a result of what he brings to it, is like a lamp that he has entrusted to Mary's care. She is the guardian of his love because she already loves. It is *given* to her because she already *has*. She is both like the rich man to whom riches are given and the poor man from whom is taken away "even that which he hath"—out of love for love, so that love may flourish. At first, love is as it were latent: the Lord, journeying here and there, is its pure, invisible radiance, and Mary is its pure, invisible expectation. Martha's action releases it into visibility, causing its hidden energy to explode.

... *and listened to his teaching*. Mary listens to the words pouring forth, she hears them in their fresh, dynamic originality. Every one of the Lord's words is stamped with this same fundamental quality: as an expression of eternally valid truth and being, each word is primal, of the fountainhead *and* at the same time in dynamic process. The Lord stands at the center of his self-revelation; out of love he continually creates new expressions of love that men can understand, and his word will be a fountain in this way until the end of the world. This is because the Lord is what he says. In receiving his word, Mary receives the Lord's being. His word nourishes her contemplation of his being, and since it is of the essence of the Son to contemplate the Father in the Spirit and to strive toward him, he develops these same proportions in Mary's contemplation too. In her, the word heard, the Word contemplated, is open to the infinity of the Divine Being in an openness that is one with love. Each partial truth that the Lord communicates to her always contains the whole of truth and love, because he puts himself into each one of his words, and as the Son he is indivisible. If we could know what is the content of Mary's contemplation, if we could see how little she knows in terms of quantity, and how little, perhaps, the Lord says to her, we would probably be amazed and deeply moved to see that it is sufficient to fill her whole inner self, her whole life. This is possible because Jesus' words contain his whole being. This may be what we are most inclined to forget: that every word of God points to the Son's indivisible being as Word, Logos; also, that nothing is created apart from this Word. This implies in turn that nothing that is or that will be is without access to God's love and word—and both his love and his word are whole and entire. God has the power to fill everything with his love and thus to satisfy created being, which is oriented to and dependent on love and the word. To adapt himself to the developmental structure of the creature, God wields his own being in the manner of organic growth, so that at all points his words of love become seeds of love within us, and the seed that sprouts and springs up is also the fulfilment of the field. All contemplative life results from a fulfilment of love taking place here and now, since God's word and being are eternally happening in love. But Martha was distracted with much serving; and she went to him and said: Lord, do you not care that my sister has left me to serve alone? Tell her then to help me. Martha goes on performing her service of love: everything she does is meant as service to the Lord. But she has made her own actions the norm of such service. And the more she has to do, the more she is contrasted with the picture of Mary, who simply listens and contemplates. This pure abiding in love is always to be found in genuine contemplation. Here there is no restless to and fro, no interruption. Distraction is as out of place in contemplative life as it is in prayer. It would mean that the connection between the contemplative and the Lord was sometimes closer, sometimes more remote. It would mean that the path was sometimes shorter and sometimes longer, so that the contemplative would be reminded, either by his inner disposition or by time or some external circumstance, that he was presently in the contemplative phase—whereas for the true contemplative there should be no going away and returning. His life and his senses are in the Lord. He lives at the Lord's feet, listening to his word, close to his being. Martha, however, is always running here and there: she invited the Lord and made it possible for her sister and him to be together. Next she is less concerned about the Lord than about his needs, and gradually it turns out that she is a better judge of his needs than he is. Her prime intention is a good one, but secondary intentions are there too, and they gain the upper hand.

There comes a time when she can see absolutely nothing but this service of hers, which has entirely taken on the form of her own wishes. The Lord, as he really is, has totally disappeared behind her view of what his needs are. Somehow she has lost hold of the essentials; instead of going directly to the Lord, she has become identified with love of the *things* of the Lord. Covertly they are transformed into things that Martha does, things she is glad to do. And all this goes on in an atmosphere of tension and anxiety arising from her being pushed beyond her limits. Thus an estrangement comes about. Martha no longer understands her sister's contemplative life. At first, when she invited the Lord into the house and Mary sat at his feet, all was well. But she disturbed this peaceful order by her over-busyness, and now she wants to create a new order along her own lines. The norm of this new order is set by her understanding of the Lord's needs and her ministering to them, and Mary too is to submit to it. Thus action is alienated from contemplation; it misinterprets both the nature of the Lord and the nature of contemplation.

She turns to the Lord, not in order to pay attention to him, but so that he shall pay attention to her and do her will. He is no longer in charge: she is. She puts into his mouth the words she wants to hear from him. Perhaps she would still grant that a certain amount of contemplation is a good thing. But perhaps contemplation is already so far away from her that she cannot see it, because she no longer understands that what the Lord requires is love and that this requirement is being fulfilled by Mary's attitude. Martha has turned things upside down. Love too has become more of an active idea, realized by deeds. This is the love Martha puts into practice, and the only way the Lord can act is to follow her, to submit to her demands. In the end he only exists to accept the form of service that action dictates. If the Lord were like this, he would only

recognize, value and promote *works*. Left to herself, without the Lord's intervention, Martha would
fashion the developing Church's *caritas* according to
her own ideas. Her manifold busyness would circle
around a moribund center; the Lord would have
become a kind of statue: continually dusted, with
candles lit before it, the centerpiece of ceremonies,
it would show no signs of life, let alone utter a sovereign word to command the attention of the min-
istrants. Such a statue would be nothing more than
an excuse for people who like to be doing things,
allowing them to live as it suits them under the pre-
text of serving God.

At first no exchange of words is recorded. The
Lord was travelling, and Martha invited him into
her house; we do not know what was said at this
first encounter. The Lord begins to speak, and Mary
listens. And Martha, going beyond her responsibil-
ities in a totally unfitting manner, interrupts him.
She interrupts prayer. Prayer time should always be
given by the Lord; he sets the quantity, duration
and intensity. For the words that are uttered here
are his words of love, gifts given out of love and
for love. To interrupt the Lord when he is speaking
with those who are his is to disregard love's mode
of operation. Every period of contemplation should
be returned to the Lord in the form of a period of
love. And Mary is only listening; she shows no sign
of tiredness (which might have been a reason for

Martha to interrupt); she is being borne up by the Word of God; there is nothing in her that requires interruption or change.

But the Lord answered her, "Martha, Martha, you are anxious and troubled about many things; one thing is necessary. Mary has chosen the best portion, which shall not be taken away from her." The Lord lets himself be interrupted, just as the Church does. It cannot be said that such interruption is the Lord's will. It lies outside his will. But he makes the best of the interruption, by using it to bring Martha back to the right path. He and Mary were in converse in the divine word: the word addressed to Martha was superfluous as far as they were concerned. Contemplation has suffered a certain setback as a result of this untimely incursion. Yet what comes from it is a most solemn and fruitful admonition to the active life, for all ages to come linking action and contemplation in a new and effective way.

The Lord shows Martha that her timetable is too full, that she is doing too much, that she is taking too much on herself. If the Lord had not called a halt, her restless activity would have drawn Mary into itself; she would even have tried to make the Lord follow her unexpressed wishes and be silent: let him stop talking so that Mary can be available for active service. If Mary is withdrawn from contemplation, the Lord too is prevented from giving the word of contemplation, for it is a word of reciprocal love, and it presupposes that the believer is listening and is a receptive vessel.

However, since Martha has not gone too far away and has ultimately good intentions, since she has faith and loves in her own way, she hears the word addressed to her—an effective word, which now takes effect in her. She hears the Lord's rebuke, but she also hears—like a reward for having accepted the rebuke—this majestic word: One thing is necessary. And she is not excluded from this one thing. But it is something that is inherent in the Lord, something created by the bond between him and Mary. This one thing resides in the totality of his love; it contains his truth, but it also reveals his relationship to men and, through it, his relationship to the Father in the Holy Spirit. The one thing can never be encompassed since it is the whole, and since the totality of truth is always one with the ineffable simplicity of God. Here, this one thing is only indicated, although the expression used clearly sets the course toward it. All the doors leading to the one thing are opened, but it is itself governed by the Lord alone; love is its abiding and exclusive context. It is this one thing that joins the Word that he is and the word that he utters, making the apparently chance word into absolute necessity. The one thing is perfectly sole and alone because it includes all community. It is one in the way God is one in his triune Being. It is the one thing that exists prior to being uttered and which is always on the verge of being uttered. It has joined Mary and the Lord, yet not in an exclusive manner; the Lord turns to Martha so that she too may be adopted into this one thing necessary and be cherished by its love.

Martha's activity is "many things", fragmentation. It is unstable, for at first it was right activity performed for the Lord, and then it became something done according to her own judgment: overbusy, piecemeal activity, all the time becoming smaller and more petty. The multiplicity of actions no longer proceeds from a unity, no longer seeks it, and so it clashes with the Lord's coming and going, which is unitary. Her activities have become directionless, taking whatever path seems good to them, upsetting the Lord and Mary, and ultimately herself as well. This work no longer has substance; it has all become scattered, peripheral. First it was concerned with the Lord's needs, then with Martha's, then with purely imaginary ones utterly foreign to Mary, but which Martha would like to foist on her. Alienation produces more alienation. It is like a man turning off a road and travelling cross country: he gets further from the road at an increasing rate, until he is completely lost. Had not Martha been restrained by the Lord's word, she would have been so enveloped by even more of her own concerns that her first intention, service, would have been completely stifled. Love would have given place to inclination, divine love to self-love.

Mary has chosen the best portion.... All that is available for our choosing is our allotted inheritance. The Lord, who is God, describes what Mary has chosen as the "best portion". And since the Lord was love from all eternity and came among men for love of them, choosing his path from beginning to end as the path of love, there is nothing he loves more than love itself. Love is the "best portion" that Mary has chosen. This love is something that comes from him. She has chosen it: in other words, there were other things she could have chosen. Her choice followed a genuine decision, an insight facilitated by love. Motivated by love, she chose love. She was motivated by a love that lived in her and came from the Lord, a love that felt as if it went through her, coming from God and going to God. For her, choosing meant offering herself freely to love, in order to pledge herself to whatever love should show her. Of her own choice she plunges into the torrent of love and lets this torrent flow through her. And out of the fulness of love she lays hold of whatever flows to her from the Lord, whatever he offers her. There is no compulsion in this love; the lover moves freely within it, freely approaches it. That is why the Lord speaks of the

choice. Mary's choice is to be chosen by the Lord.
Her choosing was an answer to the Lord's question,
an answer to a question posed by all love, and it was
in love that she found her answer. For her, choosing
meant endeavoring to speak the Lord's language.
This, for her, was the "best portion" because it is
the Lord's portion, because it is the highest thing
he has offered and given to men: namely, that, listening to his word and opened up to him, they are
given a share in his being as the Logos.

Martha, however, is being reprimanded by the
Lord. Thus he does not speak of Martha's choice.
Nor can we be certain whether Martha seriously
made a choice. His admonition to Martha ends by
pointing her to Mary. Now it is as if Martha is an
ordinary believer to whom the Lord is holding up
the excellence and holiness of Mary's chosen vocation and state of life for her to choose. She does
not have to make the same choice, but choose she
must. The Lord does not forget that he came into
the house through Martha, that it was she who
invited him and now looks after him. But Mary's
welfare is, as it were, included in his; so if Martha is
to serve, she must also serve the Mary who is doing
the Lord's work. She must not try to distract her
by her own ministry, which is not so important;
she must not try to induce Mary to leave the most
important things for the sake of the less important.
What she had in mind for Mary was fashioned after

her own image. But she did right, in her real or imagined straits, to turn, not to Mary, but to the Lord; thus she lent him an opportunity of giving the words heard by Mary a meaning for Martha as well. She allows the Lord to correct her. She has to do without the praise that she may well have expected; instead, he points to the example of her sister. She can count on Mary, but not in the way she thought: Mary will help her in whatever way she can within her choice of the "best portion". Perhaps, if Mary had helped her in the practical way Martha had intended, Martha would have done even more than she was able to do on her own. Now that Mary will not help her in that way, Martha will not do so much, but the things she does will have a share in Mary's contemplation and prayer, which draw their nourishment from that "best portion" of hers. Mary is to keep this one thing necessary, this portion. In the Lord's eyes it is the most important portion since it contains his love; he gives it, in love, to those who love him. In choosing it, Mary shows that she has a true understanding of divine love; she has taken what God most wanted to give, the love that is expressed in his becoming man and that testifies to his eternal being in the Father and the Spirit.

. . . which shall not be taken away from her. Because Mary's service belongs to God, the Lord will protect

it against Martha's attacks; Mary is to keep it, for otherwise the Lord would be the poorer. Otherwise his love would no longer be able to communicate itself in this special way; there would be no response to his question. For he has invested the deepest mystery of his Incarnation in this "portion" and needs Mary and all praying people to witness to it.

Although these words of his refer to Mary, she is not the central person; the central figure is the Lord, for it is he who needs this service of contemplation. He has need of it and deigns to accept Mary's service. By putting it under his protection, he shows that priority and precedence are governed by his needs and not man's. He, the Lord, is the One, and that is why there is "one thing necessary".

This being so, everyone must be at pains to see that Mary can perform her service in peace. To disturb her is to disturb the Lord. Martha must do what she has to do—that too is necessary in its own way—but without interrupting what is going on between the Lord and Mary, without disturbing this listening, this prayer. Such disturbance of love can only spring from what is nonlove.

Mary is also listening when the Lord is speaking to her sister. Her listening never comes to an end. Just as she listened to the words that referred to her, so now she listens to those addressed to Martha, for they too apply to her. For her own part she must acquire a proper attitude toward Martha's work, not from Martha herself but from the Lord. The Lord has Martha's life and Mary's life in his hands. But to Mary, the contemplative, all of the Lord's words belong, as many as she can lay hold of. He speaks in Mary's presence, confirms and extends her vocation, but in doing so he also allots to Martha a place of her own that will guarantee her a share in the one thing necessary, provided she does not interfere with it but lets it happen.

THE MEAL IN BETHANY

(John 12:1–8)

Six days before the Passover, Jesus came to Bethany, where Lazarus was, whom Jesus had raised from the dead. There they made him a supper; Martha served, and Lazarus was one of those at table with him. The meal in Bethany takes place very shortly before the Passion. Yet it is not the Cross that the assembled company has in view, but rather the coming kingdom, that is, Easter, prefigured in the Lazarus who has been raised from the dead. The Cross stands veiled between the present and Easter. With the anointing by Mary of Bethany it begins to reveal itself. Mary's contemplation already belongs to the Cross. The active Martha and the raised Lazarus belong more on the side of life. By sitting down to eat with them, the Lord shows that he himself is the living one: he who became man in order to live among us, and who rises again to be forever both guest and host in the meals that the Church celebrates. The whole mystery of his death is as though veiled and hidden

within his life. There they sit, his fellow guests, eating and being served. It is a day like other days, but
it has an air of festivity about it; they rejoice to be
sharing good company here and now, and Martha's
service is a symbol of the "here and now".

*Mary took a pound of costly ointment of pure nard and
anointed the feet of Jesus and wiped his feet with her
hair; and the house was filled with the fragrance of the
ointment.* Suddenly Mary interrupts the everyday
conviviality. She emerges from her contemplation
to do something quite beyond the everyday round,
an act of pure service, performed, not for men, but
for God. It is on a different level from Martha's service, which looks after the body, for Mary's concern is for the fulfilment of something that has been
promised. She undertakes it with the characteristic
assurance of the contemplative. She does something
that all those who are not contemplatives feel to
be completely out of the blue and arbitrary—and
in fact the context of her deed is only manifested
within this contemplation of the Lord.

Whereas before, when she sat at the Lord's feet,
she was inundated by his love as it streamed from
love to love, now she is in this very same stream
of love. But now, as it flows from the Father to the
Father, this torrent carves out a new bed for itself. It
awaits a new impulse that the Son, in his humanity,
is to receive from the human being, Mary, within

the life of contemplation. Mary's contemplation
and the act of anointing that stems from it will initiate the contemplation of the Cross.

Here we are presented with a new facet of love.
Mary had chosen the best portion in desiring to
live exclusively by the Lord's love, with whatever
it should send her. And now, again, she selects the
best part of her earlier choice, by deciding to chan-
nel the Son's love, which caused him to become
man, toward his return to the Father.

By listening intently to the words of Jesus she
has been so deeply initiated by him into the triune,
divine mysteries, that now she seems to receive her
instructions directly from the Father. In his name
she ministers to the Son, setting the Son and his
mission before the Father in a new way, just as
the Son had once revealed to her the Father and the
Spirit within her love-inspired choice. She has so
advanced in the art of being at God's disposal that
now it seems to be the Father's will, rather than the
Son's, which she allows to take place within her. It
is on this basis that she causes the centrality of the
Son to shine forth in a new way. It is a new mode
of revelation in the world of that life which is by
nature one and yet threefold. Without necessarily
expressing it, each divine Person shares in anticipation of what the other undertakes.

And now Mary brings the nard and anoints the
Lord's feet with it. Earlier she sat at the Lord's feet:

so now she applies herself to his feet. She uses genuine, precious ointment, which symbolizes the great price that God sets on the soul that is his gift. The Lord lives a life of poverty, yet there is nothing poor about the demands he makes!—unless poverty were to mean "everything, totally and immediately". There is a certain kind of prodigality that is found only in Christian poverty. The rich man, once he has decided to give, cannot give enough; he has so much, and having given one thing away, he discovers that he has more to give. There are simply not enough days in his life for him to give all his goods to the Lord. The poor man who has nothing or next to nothing, when he starts to give, quickly comes to the end of what he has. Once he has determined to give, he must give everything at once. He has so little that it does not make sense to split it up. But to the Lord the little he possesses and gives has the fragrance of the most precious nard, for it has the fragrance that belongs to the whole. One thing is necessary. Mary gives this one thing, the whole that she possesses, herself; in giving the nard she gives all that she has, for it is precious and signifies a person's entire possessions.

In no way does she give merely the external gift; the nard embodies herself—and yet not herself, for she gave herself away long ago. She enacts the whole movement of "giving to the Lord". In her the divine commission is embodied. The Father wants the Son

to receive the most costly gift as a prelude to the
Son's own unique and most costly mission—as a sign
of his fatherly ratification, as a pledge, as an overture
to his "hour". Mary well knows the world's time,
running out with the passing hours, but for her all
time is prayer time. And this includes times such as
mealtimes, for since she began to listen to the Lord's
words, this listening of hers will never stop. And
since she listens unceasingly, she has an understanding of eternal time. However, in the Father's eternal
time, in this commission of Mary's, the Son's hour
has struck. Something falls from heaven and enters
into the Lord's remaining days. Mary gives far more
than merely her own self: she gives the Son a sign,
coming from God's eternal time, announcing that
the hour has struck. In revealing to him something
from eternity, she is the Father's messenger, the
Father's "*Memento!*", she calls him back. His path
has come to an end; he must go home to the Father.

By anointing the Lord in view of his suffering,
Mary anoints him together with all the sinners who
hope for redemption. Mary repeats the actions of
the woman who was a sinner, who anointed the
Lord in hope and received the remission of her
sins in return. In her love she repeats the gesture
of humility. She wants to remind the Lord of that
woman: she wants him to see in her love the love
of sinners. She includes in herself all those who in
any way are nourished, here and now, by his life;

all those he has called. In her love she leads them to
him, like children who have to be brought to him
and introduced, so that he will bless them, and also
so that they shall begin to hear his word and have
a share in his vision of the Father—and so that, as a
result of Mary's action, which was inspired by
the Father as an act of love, they shall make the
time leading up to Easter into a Passiontide to prepare the way for the Son's great act of love and to
accompany him through it.

She dries his feet with her hair as the sinner had
done. Her hair becomes a towel, just as at the washing of the feet the Lord makes himself into a towel
for his disciples to use. The body of this woman is
requisitioned and made into a utensil in the Lord's
service, because the Lord will use his own body as
an instrument to redeem those who are his. It is like
a chain of redemption: it lies in the Lord's hand, but
he hands it over, link by link, so that the Father can
show it to his chosen ones and so that every hour
can find its place in the chain, and he can soon say,
"The hour is come!"

The fragrance of the ointment fills the whole
house. The nard gives off its fragrance for the Lord.
But its fragrance becomes his, so that there is in him
a single fragrance, intended for everyone. The fragrance has become apostolic. It points to the Son
who was anointed, to Mary who performed the
anointing; it connects his mission with hers and

allows the eyes of believers to catch sight of the unity he makes of himself and those who are his, which originates with his own unity with the Father in the Holy Spirit. It is a divine, triune fragrance that always indicates the Son—his mission, not his person in isolation—but at the same time it is always seen together with the mission of those who love him, with the mission of Mary, who lives through the Father by commission of the Son.

The house filled with perfume has become the area of the Church. The perfume links everyone together. It links those who are in the house, but also, somehow or other, those who may enter the house, for whom the house is waiting. Here the perfume always indicates the presence of the Son. The house would be unthinkable without this fragrance of the Lord, which is at the same time the precious perfume of the soul dedicated to the Lord. The perfume is like love: it permeates everywhere, fills everything and unites everyone.

This perfume is a very particular one: it is the fragrance of the very nard that belonged to Mary and which she used to anoint the Lord, the fragrance that "filled the whole house". Now, set free, it declares itself to all. It manifests the fruitfulness of this particular love. It leaves its vessel, the nard is poured over the Lord's feet, and the excess is taken up by Mary's hair, which in turn receives and broadcasts the fragrance. Feet and hair conspire to spread the perfume, filling the house and showing that it is a house of divine love. Mary's love has released the love kept hidden in the vessel, creating total availability. All Christian love is like this: there must be a meeting with the Lord so that love can realize itself and attain fulness. And though this love abides in contemplation, it must be a contemplation that genuinely meets the Lord, a *contemplation* within which this *action* of meeting the Lord takes place. This is so that the love can be communicated, so that it can also reach people who do not participate in it directly. It is like music: it can be written down, but if all are to share in it, it needs to be played.

But Judas Iscariot, one of his disciples (he who was to betray him), said, "Why was this ointment not sold for three hundred denarii and given to the poor?" This he said, not that he cared for the poor, but because he was a thief, and as he had the money box, he used to take what was put into it. Judas is appalled at this waste; but what really upsets him is this manifestation of love. If the ointment had been sold prior to this, all traces of it would have been removed from the scene at an early stage; this scandalous display of love would have been avoided. The vessel, which was in the house, in the Lord's immediate vicinity, would have been disposed of without performing its service to the Lord, and the proceeds could have been given to the poor, to people who, as a result, would not have come into direct contact with the Lord. Judas' plan is a plan of nonencounter, nonEucharist, non-fulfilment. Everything would have stayed as it was, and there would have been a different distribution; Judas and those like him would have had the satisfaction of feeling that they had achieved something. It would have been a *work* instead of love, a convenient substitution. It would have done away with the showing of love for its own sake, abolished the fulfilment that follows from meeting the Lord and from contact with him. "This way is just as good." This is the picture of the "good Christian" who no longer prays.

The man who keeps to himself what is due to the Lord is a thief. He thwarts the proper course of things. He puts his hand into the till, taking for his own use what is supposed to be for the Lord's work. Judas is the prototype of those people who condescend to go part of the way with the Lord but never get very far because their own ends come first: they have "kept" themselves. They satisfy their own needs, using up what was meant both for the Lord and for the brethren. Here we see the stark contrast between the eucharistic approach of the Lord and the completely egoistic approach of Judas. He stands for all those who, outwardly, seem fully to share the Lord's life, but who remain aloof, inwardly refusing to fill their lives with what is essential. Judas is their progenitor. Their Christianity is a matter of habit; they live a double existence, seeming to be what in fact they are not. Their inner life is closed to the Lord's. They go so far as to put forward their own suggestions in opposition to the Lord's, in his very presence, and yet remain within the ranks of his followers. They will not betray the Lord to his face, but inwardly they have already done so. They have managed to do the inconceivable: they have made themselves impervious to his word.

Jesus said, "Let her alone, let her keep it for the day of my burial. The poor you always have with you, but you do not always have me." The Lord approves what Mary has done. It is something that is in harmony with the will of the triune God. It is one of those deeds that has been predetermined from all eternity, that sums up a life. Mary acts as an instrument. But the Lord, having become man, must add his human approbation to the triune God's approbation of Mary's deed. The words addressed to men are also intended for God the Father in heaven, so that, from them, he will see the perfect unity of the Son's will on earth with God's will in heaven.

Let her. . . . This is spoken almost as much to the Father as to men. Jesus' consent, which Mary did not seek before performing her deed, is here made manifest to all, including the Father in heaven. It was an anointing in view of his impending burial, a

sign of and a prelude to the Passion. The Son shows
the Father that he has recognized the sign of his
approaching hour and that his human will is prepared to accept it. *Let her....* For the disciples this
means that the epoch introduced by Mary has properly started, a period in which all shall take place
in the unity of that fragrance of love that fills the
whole house. The Eucharist too will be instituted
in this same unity. What has taken place here was
an anticipatory sign of the Eucharist in its perfected
form, but also a sign of the Son's ever-perfect love
that never strays from the Father.

So these words apply both to heaven and to earth;
they are addressed both to the Father and to the disciples. But they also apply to Mary, putting on her
the seal of approval. She is given an inalienable place
in the tale of the Lord's sufferings. In her purity she
brings the Lord the heaven-sent sign of his hour.
As she pours out the vessel of ointment, she herself
becomes fully and entirely a vessel. Now her past,
which often seemed so insignificant to her, becomes
as precious and rich as the sweet-smelling perfume.
She is totally devoted to him. She has become a saint
whose whole life is exclusively mediation; she lets
the word and the will of God stream through her,
and carries out whatever is asked of her. *Let her....*
This is Jesus' affirmation that whatever Mary has to
do, she does perfectly. He also says it to reassure
her; hearing these words of approval, she knows,

after the event, that she has acted correctly. From now on, therefore—although not interested in having views about her own position—she knows that she is where the Lord wants her. She is clothed in holiness; but it does not concern her. And what she did not grasp or grasped only imperfectly while she was performing her deed she now sees with utter clarity in the Lord as a result of his ratifying words. Even if his words do not reveal to her every detail of the path that lies before him, she is assured that she is following him with proper obedience.

The poor you always have with you.... There will always be opportunities to do things in the Lord's name. As Judas shows, such deeds can be performed in external proximity to the Lord; they can evince a certain likeness to his deeds that makes them hard to distinguish—yet they completely miss the mark. They can only avoid doing this if they are inspired by the spirit that informed Mary's action.... *but you do not always have me.* It is harder to live with the Lord than to have the poor around one; harder to carry out the Lord's will than to satisfy the needs of the poor. In saying this the Lord gives contemplation its full value. He reveals a divine meaning in the encounter with him, setting himself in the highest place and giving the poor (and, with them, all others) second place. It is only the fact that he is there that lends significance to our concern for the poor, to good works and the love of neighbor. His presence has the absolute primacy over that of all others. Here again we have the one thing necessary, clearly contrasting with Martha's preoccupations and judging them. Here the one thing necessary has found expression in the divinely inspired act of Mary's pure contemplation; everything else falls into place around it, keeping a certain distance. The Lord himself determines this distance. It is the distance that both separates and unites the Creator and the creature.

The fact that the poor who are always with us are allotted second place implies no low opinion of them. All it means is that the poor can only take first place because the Lord has dwelt among us. Judas and the lukewarm who are like him will, in performing works of faith, short-circuit the Lord's mediation in their attention to the poor. They will do their own work and perhaps attribute it to the Lord, or, if their egoism happens to be shaken a little, they will call it altruism; but since they do not see the Lord in the poor, the Lord whom we do not always have with us, their altruism will have no connection with the absolute quality of divine love. In spite of the many people under their care they will not constitute the two or three who are assembled in the Lord's name so that he can dwell among them. They will not even wish it. Since they do not love him, they will create a distance between him and themselves that is not the distance the Lord intends. And the love that he, as God-made-man, has brought from heaven to earth will not envelop them, for they scorn to follow the Lord's way and the way of Mary of Bethany, preferring to follow paths of their own finding.

... *but you do not always have me*. In being a man, the Son is performing an act of love both to the Father and to men. He has become like us out of love, the triune love into which he invites men. By loving every human being, the Son creates in each the ability to love the Father and Creator with a love that is itself God-like. That love which at first seemed to be the privilege of the eternal God, streaming forth within him, proceeding from him and returning to him, is powerful enough to draw even the outer world into itself. And since the Father loves his creatures, he needs them in his loving bosom; he neither can nor will be without them in the heart of his triune love. As man, however, the Son brings his sacrifice to the Father in the form of a demonstration of love that is so strong that it can become a demonstration of love on behalf of all men as well. His love has the eucharistic power to justify and sanctify mankind. He who appeared once, uniquely, who lived and died, whom men "do not always have with them", caused all eternal love to come into the world. If he were in the world for all time, he would not be a man like other men; he could neither represent men nor be loved in his humanity by all men. Even though eternal love becomes man among men, for its incarnation to be genuine it cannot stay with us in human form for all time. This "not always" is our guarantee that it will remain with us eternally.

This presence that is only temporal—yet genuinely temporal—brings infinite blessedness (which is why the poor must take second place) because it is the expression of the Father's eternal love for his creatures, manifested in the Son. It expresses all conceivable heavenly love. This love is the one thing necessary that Mary has grasped. Mary loved exactly as was asked of her. She loved the Son given by the Father; in the Son she loved the Father, and, loving Father and Son, she loves her fellow men in the way the Son shows her. The perfume of the squandered ointment is like the fragrance of the Lord, squandered in the Eucharist. By her action Mary makes the Lord's love perceptible to all in the house. All receive some new gift, all experience a revitalization of their love for the Son and the Father, which always includes all mankind.

Mary has made the act of the sinner, which was an act of hope, into an act of fulfilment by transforming the hope for redemption into a redemptive love. But the act of hope was already rooted in Magdalen's act of faith. Faith is the beginning and the end: the beginning, because Magdalen has let herself be freed from her demons so that she can walk with the Lord; the end, because it was granted to her to be the first to believe at the tomb. And yet it is not that faith supports hope and love: love is the foundation for everything, for the Lord's love gives faith and fulfils hope. Nor does it know limitation or restriction: it issues an open invitation to all to share in loving the Father with the love of the Son.

Thus these three women have become an expression of faith, hope and love, a symbol of the triune life of the Son. Coming to earth out of love, he prodigally bestows not only his own love but also the love of the Father in the Holy Spirit. Faith and hope are the ways in which human beings can be made ready to receive the divine love; it pours itself out over them, and then the Son collects it up again and presents it to the Father as the love of his creation. The Son is the Mediator, distributing and gathering together, coming and going. What he brings with him is heavenly love; what he takes away with him is the world's love, awakened by the summons of triune love, entering into the circle of triune life.